Social Media
and South Korean
National Security

# Social Media and South Korean National Security

## Yongho Kim

McFarland & Company, Inc., Publishers
*Jefferson, North Carolina*

LIBRARY OF CONGRESS CATALOGUING-IN-PUBLICATION DATA

Names: Kim, Yong-ho, 1964– author.
Title: Social media and South Korean national security /
Yongho Kim.
Description: Jefferson, North Carolina : McFarland & Company, Inc.,
Publishers, 2017 | Includes bibliographical references.
Identifiers: LCCN 2017015396 | ISBN 9780786496877
(softcover : acid free paper) ∞
Subjects: LCSH: Mass media policy—Korea (South) | Disclosure of
information—Korea (South) | Social media—Political aspects—
Korea (South) | Civil rights—Korea (South) | National security—
Korea (South) | Military intelligence—Korea (South)
Classification: LCC P95.82.K6 K5684 2017 | DDC 302.2309519—dc23
LC record available at https://lccn.loc.gov/2017015396

BRITISH LIBRARY CATALOGUING DATA ARE AVAILABLE

ISBN (print) 978-0-7864-9687-7
ISBN (ebook) 978-1-4766-2863-9

Front cover images © 2017 iStock

Printed in the United States of America

*McFarland & Company, Inc., Publishers
Box 611, Jefferson, North Carolina 28640
www.mcfarlandpub.com*

# Table of Contents

# Preface

When I published my earlier book, *National Security, the Media and the National Assembly,* in Korean in 1999, I focused on the interaction between the media and the government, with the National Assembly, South Korea's unicameral parliamentary body, as an intervening variable. At that time, public opinion had not yet exerted significant influence on the interaction between the media and national security, although democratization increased citizen involvement in other areas of public policy regarding taxation, consumer price, housing, labor and employment. National security attracted little attention because it did not affect people's pockets compared with other issues. It was the intensified inter–Korean cooperation initiated by Kim Dae-jung's sunshine policy in the late 1990s that triggered public attention on issues regarding North Korea and national security. Then, anti–Americanism became a hotly debated issue in the presidential election in 2002, which led me to open an undergraduate course on this subject. I witnessed competition between TV news and newspapers over the framing of national security issues and saw the impact of social media in providing a conduit for individual voices.

In writing this volume, I have benefited from my personal experience as the specialist reporter on unification affairs at *Joongang Daily* in Seoul, Korea. My personal friendships with my former colleagues kept me informed of new developments within the news-making industry and provided various chances to exchange views on the role of social media. My experience as a commentator for the Korea Broadcasting Station (KBS) and TV Chosun also provided me with valuable opportunities to witness what was actually going on within the media-policy link inside the evolving environment of emerging cable news networks and social media. I am grateful for all these opportunities.

As a person specializing in international relations, I have research interests that are rather slanted toward national security, rather than toward journalism and media studies. For me, it was not easy to find a book on this subject with a balanced view between civil rights and national security. I was lucky to find Rahul Sagar's *Secrets and Leaks: The Dilemma of State Secrecy* and Darren Davis's *Negative Liberty: Public Opinion and the Terrorist Attacks on America*, both of which enlightened me to develop a balanced view between national security and civil rights. I am heavily indebted to the authors for their informative and theoretical analysis.

I have to mention my research assistants. I wish to express my gratitude to Dr. Jaeyoung Hur, who had been the principal research assistant for this project. I am pleased that he now teaches at Yonsei. But for his support and help, I would not have completed this volume. I also wish to thank Yeongjun Choi, Narae Yim, Jiseon Hwang, Seyoung Jung, Sohee Hwang, Nagyon Kim and Hwanbi Lee for providing valuable assistance. Professor Lonnie Edge also provided indispensable editorial support for making my manuscript more readable.

Financially, the National Research Foundation of Korea provided the main support for this research. This work was supported by the National Research Foundation of Korea grant, funded by the Korean government (NRF-2012S1A5A2A01014411). This research was also partially supported by the Yonsei University Research Fund. I deeply appreciate their sincerity and patience in supporting this project.

Lastly, I want to express my deepest gratitude to my late father, who provided me valuable insights on South Korea's national security by telling me stories about his personal experiences holding various governmental posts. I also wish to thank my mother, who has always been my sincere supporter. I just wish she could know how much I respect and love her. I also thank my wife and son, who always give me joy and happiness. My life owes a great deal to all of them.

# Introduction

The book probes the influence of social media on national security. Some argue that social media influence the making of security policy in an unprecedented way, exerting a critical impact. In addition, I seek to explain how variables on different levels of analysis are introduced into security policymaking, how trade-offs between security and civil liberties are affected and how messages and news stories distributed through social media differ from those reported by traditional media outlets such as newspapers and TV news. In doing so, I will focus on their impact on South Korea's policy toward North Korean provocations such as missile and nuclear tests, inter–Korean relations and the South's alliance with the United States.

Not a few have pondered the issue of media influence on national security, an area where domestic cohesion is required. Security used to be an area where citizenship was often defined in terms of "us against them," with a clear frame of what could be discussed and what could not. It has been argued that social media emerged as the third actor in government-media interaction, and subsequently that the status of newspaper and TV news as a common civic space is eroding.[1]

It is apparent that social media is gradually transforming the symbiosis between traditional media outlets and the government, with social media serving as a shortcut to information and heuristic cues.[2] Citizens gradually base their opinions on an often inaccurate representation of what social media says about national security and North Korea. The credibility of media messages depends on their sources, such as newspapers, TV news, the internet and social media, as well as the context the messages are delivered in.

Quite often, there is inconsistency between government announcements and social media descriptions of specific security events. Opinions and rhetoric expressed in social media compete with official government announcements, thereby creating situations in which the citizenry debate, choose sides and make social-media-manufactured "truth" more credible than information released by the government. Sometimes, social media over-represents negative and critical coverage of security.[3]

This book introduces social media in national security as the third actor in media-government relations through analyzing several of the cases mentioned above. Doing so illuminates media influence in ideological conflicts involving anti–Americanism, unification and North Korea's provocations. Social media plays an important role by influencing ideological differences about national security that distinguish young and old, haves and have-nots, pro–American and anti–American feeling, security and nationalism, and, finally, pro–North Korea and anti–North Korea sentiment.

This volume first introduces and develops theoretical debates over the correlation between the media and national security. In particular, this volume focuses on such issues as conflict between civil liberties and censorship relating to security, the effect of frames or framing on intentional and unintentional distortion, and the consequent media contribution to ideological debates in South Korean society.

## Why South Korea?

South Korea offers a unique set of circumstances for probing the relationship between social media and national security. First of all, the Cold War still exists on the peninsula with the increased threat from a nuclearized North Korea. All young male citizens must fulfill compulsory military duty which sees them serve at least two years in the military. In addition, the sinking of the ROKS *Cheonan* and the bombing of Yeonpyeong Island reminded the South Korean public of individual mortality in a more salient and cognitively accessible way by making North Korean attacks a part of real life.[4]

Still, it is ironic to see how conflict with North Korea triggers an increased number of ideological and bipartisan debates, unlike in many other countries, where bipartisan debate over domestic issues may be diffused by external crises.[5] In South Korea, democratization in the 1990s and the spread of mobile communication in the 2000s have invited social media into the discussion of security issues, which were once regarded as a sacred realm only allowed for the "Men in Black"—professional security specialists in relevant government sectors. Democratization has invited more citizens into the discussion of what constitutes public good and national interests, and consequently has introduced more actors into the policymaking process.

As a result, nothing is as controversial as the debate between conservatives and liberals in today's South Korea. The debate seems to be the standard issue used to draw distinctions between young and old, haves and have-nots, pro–American and anti–American and pro–North Korean and anti–North Korean camps, and, in the end, traditional media outlets and social media. This implies a gradual decrease of government influence in controlling the flow of information regarding national security and an increase of media influence in the making of foreign and security policies. Because of the ideological consciousness guiding social and political behavior, liberals and conservatives in South Korea are more likely to gravitate toward others in their in-groups. The juncture between democratization and continued confrontation with North Korea magnifies the cognitive cleavage over ideological differences, while another juncture between globalization and democratization has brought citizens into the discourse of what constitutes national interest.

Second, South Korea offers a unique theater where traditional media outlets compete with social media to attract public attention and attain credibility. While traditional and often conservative media outlets are armed with quotations and statements by high-ranking officials, the social media carry comments and opinion of citizen activists, opposition leaders and celebrities.

As noted, the spread of social media in the 2000s enlarged citizen involvement in national security. Briefings and information provided by the government are challenged by non-expert netizens who post, blog and tweet their opinions in cyberspace. Social media users in South Korea are accustomed to getting news more from the new media than from traditional media outlets. Different standards in story gate-keeping and editorial filtering often lead to behind-the-scenes stories that would not be printed or aired in traditional media outlets. Then, traditional media outlets quote stories uploaded and spread by social media. Reporting stories that other media outlets would not, and most of the time could not, has made social media niche-oriented. Social media aim to attract a smaller and more loyal audience.[6]

Social media users seldom shift their opinions after exposure to traditional media outlet reports. Rather, they tend to be driven more by opinions and arguments extended in social media. Ideologically friendly messages are more easily received than messages that are perceived as ideologically hostile. In addition, individuals seldom change their pre-existing viewpoints after official government announcements. As a result, they appear less willing to trust government announcements that are at odds with their prior views.[7] This is how such issues as the sinking of the ROKS *Cheonan*, the shelling of Yeonpyeong Island, the importation of U.S. beef and the FTA with the United States have triggered ideological cleavages embedded in public opinion.

## *Traditional Media Outlets*
## *Versus Social Media*

Modern technology has made it possible for today's media to wield a powerful and important influence on national security. In particular, social media conveys stories faster than official reporting by most governments and traditional media outlets. This has created a fast-forward effect by accelerating the speed of information delivery. Humanitarian concerns distributed and then magnified through social media may circumvent government decisions about war.

We can find several differences between traditional media outlets and social media. First, stories produced by social media are grounded in a culture friendlier to the younger generation, who know how to access and use social media. While journalists command the dominant repertoire, the social media produce unique cultural repertoires that are more easily received by the younger generation. In addition, intermittent mentions of student demonstrations and government repression in the 1980s attract those in their 40s and early 50s.[8]

Second, cultural repertoires presented by social media are not static. Rather, they themselves evolve over time amongst diverse cultural repertoires. In this process, social media deploys frames that may continuously produce stories faster than traditional media outlets.[9] Selective exposure to social media and selective attention by the younger generation may make a certain story more salient even while the older generation pays little attention to the subject.

Third, unlike traditional media reporters who are motivated by professional incentives and commercial norms, bloggers and Twitter users who express their opinions on social media are strategic. Social media are not restrained by gate-keeping norms and profit-making mechanisms. Traditional media operate under two intrinsic norms: commercial profit making and professional gate keeping with accompanying reliability checking. While pressure for profit making encourages sensational stories, gate-keeping norms morally stipulate the verification of both the source and facts. This prevents traditional media from reporting unconfirmed stories. On the contrary, social media may carry unconfirmed and often sensational stories faster than traditional media outlets.

Fourth, social media are far more effective in mass mobilization. It is argued that social media have a detrimental impact on political engagement because they distract citizens, as such media are primarily used for entertainment. However, by reducing the cost of accessing information and at the same time offering convenient ways to express opinions, social media invite not only those interested and knowledgeable but also politically inactive citizens into the process of security policymaking.[10] Social media also reduce the cost of connecting people by overcoming obstacles that were once thought to be surmountable only through bureaucratic involvement or social movement.[11] The rapid expansion of social media has opened up a cyberspace in which activists exchange dissident content that was once restricted and unavailable in off-line spaces.[12] New online opportunities for expression promote identifying and organizing like-minded citizens into a network.

Selective exposure and attention create unique environments for linking individuals into a network, which generates a mass psychology of misperception that the members are supported by unspecified groups of people within their network. Due to anonymity and mass psychology, an increase in online communication results in a higher possibility of forming bipolarity in public opinion, while an increase in off-line communication generates the opposite. According to South Korean research, only 58.8 percent of Twitter users and 78.4 percent of Facebook users in South Korea opened accounts under their real names. The same research indicates 84.1 percent of those in their 20s, 76.6 percent of those in their 30s and 74.1 percent of those in their 40s use their real name on the web. In this sense, social media are not just communication tools. They are political interpreters that form public perceptions of national security. Self-presentation on Facebook is itself a Machiavellian objective-oriented persuasion strategy full of calculated deception and lies.[13]

## Competition for the Control of Public Opinion

In the past, competition over the control of public opinion was between government officials and reporters from the traditional media outlets. In this competition for politicizing and manipulating public perceptions, the government enjoyed an information advantage of access to raw data, while the media were able to frame and prime stories, sometimes independent of the true nature of what really happened.

Symbiosis between reporters and officials assumes a far more complicated pattern in the era of social media. Traditional symbiosis between reporters and government officials for juicy bits of information and favorable coverage is now no longer valid. Social media messages appear more powerful in generating agenda-setting and priming effects that play critical roles in the approval ratings of leaders and political candidates. As an intervening actor, social media continuously brings in new citizen actors and views that are independent from the government and traditional media norms. Social media are free and accessible by citizens from various socioeconomic classes, who create Facebook and Twitter accounts, link and retweet stories and upload videos to YouTube. Through this "low-risk activism" or "slacktivism," they may create the illusion that "they are doing something meaningful." Most social media users responded positively when asked to describe their experience of using social media in one word, and only one in five responded negatively.[14]

Just as newspaper editors and network news desks prefer stories that involve mostly authoritative and high-ranking sources,[15] social media choose to tackle security issues because, in doing so, citizen activists can involve government officials as counterparts. They can upload unexpected and inconsistent messages criticizing high-ranking officials. In this process, cheap talk by celebrities and NGO leaders with little professional knowledge on national security attracts more attention and receives more public endorsement than official messages.

Social media played a key role in unfolding critical moments during the Jasmine Revolution by prompting collective action, limiting state repression, prompting international support and affecting public opinion. As a result, online activism in the Jasmine Revolution demonstrated the possibility of innovative social movements as an integral and driving component of communication.[16]

The rise of social media as an influential source of news leaves little choice but for traditional media outlets to produce more and more sensational news stories on the one hand and to rebroadcast stories generated by the social media on the other. What is defined as "reality" by social media attracts attention from traditional media outlets, thereby extending critical influence on policymaking. Rebroadcasting of such social media reports also satisfies traditional news criteria because a story from an SNS source makes it possible to get around gate-keeping norms of reliability checking.

However, social media is far from replacing the role played by traditional media, as shown in the Jasmine Revolution. The rise of social media was possible only within the context constructed by such traditional media as Al Jazeera. It was Al Jazeera that integrated various messages conveyed by social media and cultivated citizen journalists. Citizen journalists distributed news through social media, which was then rebroadcasted by Al Jazeera.[17]

## A Brief Literature Review

Most academic work focuses on the role of the media in domestic political procedure such as elections and public opinion, with only a few works dealing with the media's influence on national security. Among them, Cohen and O'Heffernan probed the subject of media and foreign policy. *The Press and Foreign Policy* by Bernard Cohen (Princeton University Press, 1963) was a pioneering classic in this field. Cohen focused on the symbiosis between diplomats and journalists in which the press actively participated in policy-making through competition and cooperation in its "love and hate relationship" (p. 147) with government officials. It is also notable that Cohen underlined the role of Congress. After nearly 30 years, Cohen's concept of symbiosis was developed into a new model called "co-evolution of mutual exploitation" by Patrick O'Heffernan in his work, *Mass Media and American Foreign Policy* (Ablex, 1991). O'Heffernan focused on government officials' deliberate use of the media in the process of policymaking as he introduced the "insider model." In doing so, he portrayed a co-evolutionary process between journalists' outside impact and deliberate leaks by officials on the inside to manipulate policy outcomes.

Cohen and O'Heffernan made indispensable contributions to the study of media-security links by introducing the media as an intrinsic actor in the policymaking process. The media, once regarded as an extrinsic actor outside the decision-making process, now interacts with other actors and intervenes in the process of molding public opinion on certain policy issues. Contributions made by Cohen and O'Heffernan have gone through further development since parachute journalism and the CNN effect brought about revolutionary changes in the pattern of news coverage in the Gulf War.

By that point, CNN had arrived. *War and the Media: Propaganda and Persuasion in the Gulf War* by Philip Taylor (Manchester University Press, 1992) is one of only a few studies that illuminated the CNN effect. This book demonstrated the unprecedented role played by CNN in the war, in which parachute journalism and fast processing of news stories evolved a totally new symbiosis. In particular, this book also introduced the other side of the coin—that is, terrorist use of the media, which ignited hotly debated issues related to civil liberties and security. The discussion of how the CNN effect brought changes to the symbiotic yet mutually exploitative relations between the media and government spurred the following research. *Taken by Storm: The Media, Public Opinion, and U.S. Foreign Policy in the Gulf War* (University of Chicago Press, 1994), edited by W. Lance Bennett and David Paletz, focused on an approach-avoidance relationship of interdependence between policymakers and journalists. The volume laid the early foundations for the discussion of the role of social media on security by looking at the diverse impacts of the media's unprecedented coverage of the Gulf War, such as "transmission of on-the-spot, more or less accurate information instantaneously worldwide, often requiring instant reactions from leaders and officials and opportunities for foreign representatives including 'enemy' spokespersons to voice their viewpoint" without the financial burden of psychological warfare (pp. 287–289).

War stories from fast-spreading network news now compete with the characterization of national security generated by social media. Quite often, social media makes a specific policy look very vulnerable through inaccurate representation of relevant facts, making the resulting opinions the most believable option in the absence of competing alternatives. In addition, the involvement of social media in the creation of security policy and the exposure of otherwise classified content to the public increase the inflexibility of security policies and their creators. *Selling Fear: Counterterrorism, the Media and Public Opinion* by Robert Shapiro et al. (University of Chicago Press, 2011) spotlights the role of the media in effectively molding public opinion for facilitating counterterrorism policies. The authors introduce the media as a political manipulator in the mass-mediated politics of counterterrorism by focusing on the Bush administration's deliberate use of the media to "sell" the war and associated fear. *Framing Terrorism: The News Media, the Government and the Public* by Pippa Norris et al. (Routledge, 2003) is another volume focusing on how different frames on terror elicit different public responses. In particular, the authors compare contradictions demonstrated by the American media and their Arabian counterparts in framing terrorism and their impact on public opinion.

Matthew Baum and Tim Groeling, in their book *War Stories: The Causes and Consequences of Public Views of War* (Princeton University Press, 2010), delineate how the media form public opinion about war, with a focus on the influence of high-level rhetoric expressed on TV talk shows under various bipartisan circumstances. The authors test a variety of hypotheses relating to high-level bipartisan rhetoric regarding the president and his war decisions. Baum and Groeling's volume is very informative in two ways. First, the study deals with the correlation between high-level descriptions of war and the degree of public endorsement of war, which is exactly what this volume will cover. Second, the authors present a range of empirical data and statistical analyses that offers exemplary guidance on how to design data analysis for this project. The Tables and Figures section also suggests methodological hints in measuring the influence of social media and traditional media outlets on security policymaking in South Korea.

*The News about the News: American Journalism in Peril* by Leonard Downie Jr. and Robert G. Kaiser (Vintage, 2003) presents its criteria for "good journalism" and "bad journalism," which is a critical standard for determining the contribution of social media to security. According to the authors, good journalism holds communities together in times of crisis by delivering information and images that encourage community cohesiveness (p. 4 and p. 265). They further indicate that bad journalism fails to report important news or deals with it in a shallow way, thereby leaving people "uninformed" of the dangers they may encounter. These failures have included media that neglected to alert the public to the dangers arising from the bankruptcy of the corrupt savings and loan industry or the addictive and cancer-causing effects of smoking (p. 6). The authors also forecast the bad effects of social media "delivery devices" using new technologies, —including the distortion of facts and the misleading of the public as part of powerful real-time coverage of events by networked news services (p. 10 and p. 256).

The juncture of globalization and democratization brought about changes in news reporting on security, from how to conceal security to what to say about security, according to David Paletz and John Ayanian in *Communicating Politics: Mass Communications and the Political Process,* edited by Peter Golding et al. (Holmes & Meier, 1986). Security became a favored campaign tool. *Campaigning for Hearts and Minds: How Emotional Appeals in Political Ads Work* (University of Chicago Press, 2006) by Ted Brader is a valuable volume for reference in this context because it delineates an indispensable part of the role played by social media in security. It shows how emotional appeals embedded in political ads manipulate viewers' perception of security. The author demonstrates the stark difference in public response to fear ads and unimpassioned ads. In particular, the author hints that even the most "sophisticated" media users may be manipulated through social media with emotional contents (p. 183). *Political Communication and SNS* (Nanam, 2012), edited by the Korean Society for Journalism and Communication Studies, is a collection of papers written in Korean by South Korean scholars researching the political impact of SNS. Although no single chapter deals with security, the chapters provide information on the newest developments related to the impact of SNS on South Korean politics. In particular, Part II conveys helpful insights by dealing with the impact of SNS on the political process and elections. The "non-institutional political participation" through SNS that makes it harder to distinguish the private lives of individuals from socio-political participation (pp. 135–137) is also present in the realm of security. Once regarded as the exclusive area of security professionals, the issue of security in South Korea brings more and more non-professional ordinary citizens into the debate on how to deal with North Korea. The volume further indicates that a weakening of orthodox political parties and the emergence of "issue-parties" were facilitated by SNS.

*Projections of Power: Framing News, Public Opinion, and U.S. Foreign Policy* by Robert Entman (University of Chicago Press, 2004) compiles Entman's arguments on framing into a single volume. In addition to his previous arguments on the role of framing in media coverage of foreign affairs, Entman focuses on the competition between the media and elites over the control of the overarching frame. In so doing, he hints at a continuation of elites' competition with the media into a new phase of competition between social media and policymaking elites. He elaborates that the end of the Cold War paradigm made public responses to security less predictable, which increased the influence of the media (p. 21). *Who Leads Whom? Presidents, Policy, and the Public* by Brandice Canes-Wrone (University of Chicago Press, 2006) does not deal directly with media-security links. However, by elaborating on the correlation between presidents and their need for public support, the volume provides sufficient theoretical and empirical cues. In particular, the volume suggests that social media could serve as a critical political tool for presidents in maneuvering public opinion with regard to approval/disapproval ratings (pp. 86–88). *The Myth of the Rational Voter: Why Democracies Choose Bad Policies* (Princeton University Press, 2007) by Bryan Caplan offers a better understanding of how distorted stories on security elicit public attention and endorsement by raising the issue of "rational irrationality" (Ch. 5). The author explains that the desire for truth clashes with material self-interest, social pressure with conformity. He also brings up mixed cognitive motives, which facilitates our understanding of how social media maneuver public response and trigger public anger on certain security issues. *When the Press Fails: Political Power and the News Media from Iraq to Katrina* (University of Chicago Press, 2007) by W. Lance Bennett et al. focuses on "Washington political culture," which is relevant to the discussion of social media's influence on security. Social media spin the issues and intimidate the public in their coverage of security. This volume hints that a new pattern of interaction deserves scholarly attention in order to better describe the influence of social media on security. The authors indicate that social media disrupts the culture of consensus between journalists and their sources (p. 132).

Yet, scholars have not yet presented a solid analysis of the relationship between social media and policymaking elites. In addition, competition between social media and traditional media outlets over the control of framing and public attention requires further observation and analysis.

The beginning of this volume deals with various issues such as conflict between national security and civil liberties and the role of the National Assembly, South Korea's parliamentary body, in relations between national security and the media. In addition, legal judgments by the court on the issue are also examined. Chapter 1 shows that the decision to support civil liberties or national security is very situational because, in South Korea, it depends on such situational variants as North Korea's armed provocations, nuclear and missile tests, as well as peaceful gestures and inter–Korean dialogue. In the face of grave dangers to national security, citizens usually acquiesce to government authority that requires public tolerance of restrictions on civil liberties. Chapter 2 explores how the National Assembly performs its legal responsibility of oversight over national security. In particular, this chapter scrutinizes two contrasting views on the parliamentary handling of sensitive military secrets. The first view indicates that the National Assembly performs its constitutional duty as watchdog through its audit and oversight capability. The other view spotlights the lack of professional knowledge of the intelligence sector in the government by painting the National Assembly and its members as amateur and undisciplined leakers. Chapter 3 deals with legal aspects of national security and court decisions on the issue. This chapter introduces the process by which military secrets were redefined during democratization in the 1990s. It also contributes to the study of national security and the media by reviewing various legal cases that involved conflict between national security and civil rights in the United States and South Korea.

The volume then moves to analyze media influence on the creation of foreign and security policy in South Korea, and compares the influences of various media companies with differing ideological stances. Chapter 4 starts with the turning point in relations between the media and national security in South Korea, examining the junctures between post–Cold War culture and continued confrontation with North Korea on the one hand and between globalization and democratization on the other. The lifting of the perceptional taboo that had prohibited open discussion on national security was accompanied by a gradual decrease of government control over information flow on national security. In addition, a comparison among media types—press, TV, internet and social media—in their respective influences on policymaking probes the evolutionary transition of government-media relations. Chapter 5 deals with the involvement of citizens who post, blog and tweet their opinions about foreign and security affairs. Citizens are now capable of spreading their own independent ideas and weakening the symbiosis between reporters and officials. As social media gradually replaces the role of the opinion leaders and elites who used to lead public opinion, there has been a simultaneous increase in ideational confusion of the enemy/friend classification. Chapter 6 explores several sensitive cases that have attracted public engagement and media attention in South Korea: North Korean provocations, anti–Americanism and anti–Japan sentiment. The sinking of the ROKS *Cheonan* and the shelling of Yeonpyeong Island are two exemplary cases, since the South Korean public has demonstrated an ambivalence that ranges between sympathy and antagonism over continued provocations. G.I. crimes against female victims, pressure surrounding trade deals and the perception of inequality have all triggered anti–Americanism.

# 1

# Civil Liberty
# and National Security
## *A Theoretical Review*

The decision to support civil liberties or national security is extremely situational. Introduction of various security measures at airports after 9/11 demonstrated how situations determine preference between two seemingly contrasting values. Heightened security measures that were in conflict with privacy rights were justified in the name of collective security against terrorist threats. Right after 9/11, few raised objections to such security measures. However, as time went by, calls for the protection of privacy rights increased.

In South Korea too, this theme remains very situational, although confrontation with its northern counterpart has continued for more than six decades. Whether to support civil liberties or to accept the decision to restrict civil rights in the name of national security is dependent on such situational variants as North Korea's armed provocations and nuclear and missile tests, as well as peaceful gestures and inter–Korean dialogue. In the face of grave dangers to national security, citizens usually acquiesce to government authority that requires public tolerance of restrictions on civil liberties. Likewise, upon encountering various signs of easing tension with Pyongyang, citizens ask for more civil liberties. Support for concessions on civil liberties is determined at the point of compromise between perceptions of threats and democratic values such as the right to know about what really happened.

Up until the early 1990s, confrontation with North Korea had long been the excuse for authoritarian military regimes to restrict civil rights. Democratization has failed to remove many barriers that stood for national security. Moreover, support for concessions on civil liberties weakens as perception of the threat from North Korea diminishes. Accordingly, concessions relating to the right to know receive less support. Theoretically, surrender of some portion of civil liberties by empowering political authorities is a means to enhance national security, and ultimately to further citizens' liberty and freedom. In this sense, individual liberty and national security are not supposed to clash. In theory, at least, they are not mutually exclusive.[1] Nevertheless, relations between civil liberty and security are often described as mutually exclusive.

The basic idea of Rousseau's social contract lies in the concession of individual liberties to general authority in pursuit of safety. However, doing so leaves individuals under the threat of excessive exercise of authority at the expense of individual liberties. Support for freedom or liberty is situational and relative because strong supporters of liberty may become strong antagonists of liberty under certain circumstances. They are not absolute values and, indeed, are located between complete freedom and complete government control. This is why political tolerance and democratic norms are not incompatible. Public preferences between the two do not have to be politicized.[2]

In South Korea, there is growing skepticism among antigovernment activists that government authorities may be providing only selected bits of confidential information that supports their preferred policy alternatives.[3] They believe unauthorized disclosures enhance democratic accountability if they succeed in drawing public attention to potential violations of government authority and in providing citizens with the information they need to ascertain government responsibility. It is asserted that unauthorized disclosures protect civil liberties when they expose excessive use of government authority that violates individual rights.

In this chapter, an introduction of the debate between civil rights and political tolerance in the unique South Korean context is in order. Political tolerance is different from general forms of tolerance to wrongdoing by individuals. The concept of political tolerance implies tolerance of governmental intrusions on civil liberties. It heavily depends on the free will of citizens and at the same time on their perception of threats to national security.[4]

The increased influence of social media ignites debate between two conflicting principles: political tolerance for national security and democratic norms for civil liberties. On the trade-off between civil liberties and security, three main theoretical frameworks offer different explanations. The value trade-off approach suggested by Sguiv Hadari indicates that the two values are not necessarily incompatible. This approach argues against the utopian idea that the two values do not clash at all and makes it clear that it is almost impossible to weigh the two. The value pluralism model argues that trade-offs between the two depend on situational variants. When core values collide with each other and a simple solution is not apparent, citizens turn to values that require greater cognition. Terror management theory shows how emotional consequences of threat perception lead to support for authoritative restraints on civil liberties.[5]

The pattern of trade-offs between civil liberties and security in South Korea also has experienced great change. Here, personal preference for civil liberties or tolerance for national security depends on an individual's disposition, national pride and individual opinion on North Korea. Conservatives appear more sensitive to negatively framed messages and to the feasibility of worst-case scenarios. Liberals extend their view on social trust to North Korea and do not regard concession in inter–Korean negotiations as a defeat. When faced with North Korean provocations, citizens tend to concede some civil liberties for national security; however, their concessions do not last long. As other events that attract public attention arise, public perception of threats diminishes and the public need for civil liberties increases. Here, the term "negative liberty" is relevant. Negative liberty refers to the idea that minimal personal freedom or a set of rights that are free from any external or governmental interference should exist. This idea implies that civil liberties are not absolute or tradable for the benefit of security. In the United States, when the need for security overrides democratic norms of civil liberty, many democratic norms turn into practical restraints on civil liberty.[6]

When national security and fundamental democratic values clash, a democratic society faces a trade-off dilemma between the survival of its citizenry and freedom of the press—that is, citizens' right to know. Free press without doubt is an indispensable element, and the people's right to know should be respected because government decisions in crisis may generate grave consequences for the country and its citizens. On the other hand, most military operations require strict confidentiality not only for the success of the operations but also for the lives of the soldiers in them. This is why press restraint is prioritized in situations involving wars, major operations or anticipated attacks.

There are three traditional approaches in dealing with this dilemma. The most common is the "formal censorship" approach. It assumes legislation that permits prior censorship and stipulates penalties for violations. This approach focuses on the discretion of official censors to determine the sensitivity of particular information under specific circumstances. The opposite is the "free press" approach, which focuses on journalists' autonomous judgments on accepting government guidelines when deciding whether to report or hold back publication of a certain story. In this, journalists make the ultimate decision free from government requests or pressure. The third approach is "informal censorship," which assumes voluntary and selective press cooperation with no censorship laws. Informal censorship may also be labeled self-censorship.

After 9/11, the United States government developed a step-by-step manual that set forth certain principles to balance civil liberties and censorship for security reasons. The principles were designed to determine who was responsible for trade-off decisions in a diverse range of situations. In imminent wartime situations, for example, media executives, Homeland Security personnel and National Security Council staff form a joint body to define the situation, problem and range of censorship.

## Trade-Offs Between Civil Liberties and National Security

It is interesting to note that decisions to restrict civil rights have not always been made by undemocratic governments under undemocratic rulers. Abraham Lincoln was among those who suspended civil liberties by restricting the freedom of speech and the press in 1861 by banning acts that discouraged enlistment and other disloyal activities. He also suspended the writ of habeas corpus and related freedoms for similar reasons. In 1798, to silence criticisms toward President John Adams's federalist policies, his administration imprisoned and deported American citizens in the run-up to a war with France. In the 1920s, during the Palmer Raids, the U.S. government suspended the rights of communists and socialists in order for them to be arrested or deported. In 1942, Franklin D. Roosevelt ordered the detention of more than 120,000 Japanese Americans for three years. They were placed in prison camps due to fears of sabotage and treason. It was also during this period that the Smith Act authorized fingerprinting and registration of aliens in the United States. The 1950s witnessed McCarthyism and its suppression of the First Amendment rights of communists. In the 1960s, during the Vietnam War, operations by military intelligence and the CIA targeted war protestors, and President Richard Nixon even attempted to silence media criticism. From 1956 to 1971, the FBI

Counterintelligence Program (COINTELPRO) restricted the exercise of First Amendment rights of speech and association, leading to false imprisonments.[7]

In 1977, the municipal board of Skokie, Illinois, enacted ordinances to ban demonstrations portraying criminality and inciting hostility toward a person or group of persons "by reason of reference to religious, racial, ethnic, national or regional affiliation." Skokie, originally founded by Germans, was the largest community of Holocaust survivors outside of New York City. When the National Socialist Party of America attempted a Nazi march through the town, Jewish residents were not only horrified but infuriated, and the board passed legal injunctions to block the demonstration. The ban signified that demonstrations involving criminality, depravity, violence, hostility, hatred and abuse for reasons of "religious, racial, ethnic, national or regional affiliation" could be banned in the same way as demonstrations causing imminent danger to security or a substantial breach of the peace. Riots, disorder and illegal use of physical force were banned.[8]

Most Koreans seem to have no opinion when asked about their preference between civil liberties and national security. However, when asked about specific civil liberty issues or about North Korean provocations that affect daily life, they demonstrate immediate interest and express explicit favor. Commitment to civil liberties and democratic norms is hardly applicable when it collides with national security because this conflict may influence people's threat perception.[9]

It is almost impossible to choose between two or more competing values. As noted before, Hadari's value trade-off model acknowledges a certain level of incommensurability by mentioning that a lack of clashing values is only possible in a utopia. When values do collide, people tend to ignore issues easily in order to resolve conflicts. Ambivalence implies a lack of ideological constraints because conservatives and political liberals have a stronger tendency than other groups to prioritize national security or civil liberties. Ideological ambivalence also means behavioral ambivalence between ignoring problematic value conflicts and undertaking action to lower the tensions.[10]

What is unique in South Korea is that the perception of threat exerts more influence than the practical assessment of military threat. More than a few scholarly works indicate that the perception of threat is a natural byproduct of any attack or provocation. Gibson and Gouws (2003) distinguished between sociotropic threats and egocentric threats, the former referring to threats to the larger society and political order, the latter referring to threats to the individual.[11]

In general, people's perception appears to be more sensitive to egocentric threats than to sociotropic threats. This is why even in crisis situations citizens seldom give up their basic rights. Demonstrations during the Vietnam War clearly showed that repressive government policies toward civil liberties were unrelated to individual-level support for civil liberties.[12]

In the 1950s and 1960s, Korea witnessed overwhelming sociotropic threat perception caused by North Korea's frequent provocations and terrorism.[13] Then, the authoritarian regimes in the 1970s and 1980s tended to use threats from North Korea as a political means to justify suppression of opposition leaders and restrictions on civil rights. Student activists who studied Marxist-Leninist ideas and the personality cult of Kim Il Sung faced criminal charges on the basis of the National Security Law. In some cases, antigovernment demonstrations were also regarded as threats to national security and thus as pro–North Korean behavior.

Living with the North Korean threat for more than 60 years since the end of the Korean War gradually immunized people. As a result, civil liberty issues such as the right to know and trust in government compete with conservative priorities relating to patriotism and national security.[14]

The juncture between democratization and continued confrontation with North Korea magnified cognitive cleavage over

ideological differences, while another juncture between globalization and democratization has brought citizens into the discourse
of what constitutes national interest. This implies a gradual decrease
of government influence in controlling the flow of information
regarding national security and foreign affairs, and a corresponding
increase of media influence in the making of foreign and security
policies. Democratization has invited more citizens into the discussion of what constitutes public good and national interests. Consequently, more actors have been brought into the policymaking
process.

Because of the ideological consciousness guiding social and
political behavior, liberals and conservatives in South Korea are
more likely to gravitate toward others in their in-groups. It is ironic
to see that conflict with North Korea triggers more ideological and
bipartisan debates in South Korea, whereas in most countries bipartisan debate over domestic issues may be diffused by external
crises.[15] Nothing is as controversial as the debate between conservatives and liberals in today's South Korea. This debate seems to be
the standard used to draw distinctions between young and old,
haves and have-nots, pro–American and anti–American and pro–
North Korea and anti–North Korea factions and, in the end, traditional media outlets and social media.

September 11 drove the George W. Bush administration to
launch a series of measures to revive the American sense of patriotic
deference, to control the content of media reports and to silence
elite dissent in pursuit of the ultimate goal of reducing public dissent toward the war against terror.[16] Likewise, North Korean provocations such as the sinking of the ROKS *Cheonan,* the shelling of
Yeonpyeong in 2010, and nuclear tests and missile launches have
made a North Korean attack more salient and accessible by increasing the sense of vulnerability and making it a "pervasive part of
reality." Under these circumstances, South Koreans tend to support hard-line policies and at the same time gravitate toward
the government instead of criticizing it.[17] Perceptions of threats

make the amygdala, the command center that controls fear in the human brain, force the rest of the brain to focus on the source of concern by shifting brain functions away from less emergent roles such as digestion or immunity. Perceptions of threats increase decision makers' need to receive incoming information. Meanwhile, cognitive function becomes impaired and sense of judgment deteriorates.[18] Ideological conservatives appear more sensitive to negative frames, possibility of loss and salience of mortality. They appear more sensitive to personal security concerns, as North Korea's provocations remind them of the possibility of another war.[19]

However, in South Korea, security as a general issue does not receive more consistent support than civil rights that are regarded as absolute values. Ideological consciousness among liberals appears to be stronger than patriotic fervor on national security. It is not the real assessment of threat but attitudinal mindsets that influence how citizens react to government measures against North Korea's provocations. These attitudes either promote or weaken support for government policy toward North Korea. When emotional patriotism appeals, civil liberty retreats, not because of thorough analysis of situations but due to a temporary reaction that is supposed to subside as threat perception diminishes. In this case, no real change of threat exists as the resulting reaction reflects attitudinal changes.[20]

That is why the execution of Jang Song-taek exerted more influence in forming negative public perception toward North Korea than the sinking of the *Cheonan* and the shelling of Yeonpyeong Island. Public anger as well as threat perception were diminished by debates over who/what really sank the ROKS *Cheonan* and what caused North Korea to fire its artillery. Opposition party members in the National Assembly and liberals perceived threats differently than did conservatives. They raised doubts about official announcements by arguing that the sinking resulted from other causes such as a rock, shallow bottom or undersea canyon, and that the shelling resulted from South Korea's artillery drill, conducted despite repeated warnings from North Korea. However, the brutal killing of Jang Song-taek, who was believed to be in the process of opening North Korea's closed gates, left no room for defending Kim Jong-un, as it clearly showed a lack of respect for human life.

In sum, trust in governmental authority, threat perception and personal faith in civil liberties form different contexts that compete with each other to shape "the direction and magnitude" of trade-offs between national security and civil liberties. Preferences are affected by various ideological, social, economic and domestic contexts. When their attitudes are challenged, most citizens appear to harden their preexisting beliefs rather than to moderate them, although those citizens who prioritize civil liberties are more likely to moderate their positions than those who prefer national security. Lack of trust in government does not induce citizens to cede their civil rights even in the presence of a heightened sense of vulnerability.[21]

## Military Secrecy and Unauthorized Leaks

Attitudes on unauthorized leaks in South Korea present a very different picture compared to other democratic countries. What was unique in the past was a higher degree of public tolerance of government control of information on national security. Today, we have seen how the North Korean threat does not always prompt deference and unconditional loyalty to government authority. One example where military secrecy conflicted with the people's right to know in South Korea was the refusal of the military authority to permit media access to the Zaytun camp in Iraq, where South Korean troops had been stationed since August 2004. The military refused to permit media access and to provide information about the camp, which could allegedly jeopardize the safety of the troops. The refusal was a contrast to the embedding program operated on

American bases in spite of dozens of soldiers killed in action every month.

In the United States, too, governmental authority usually prioritizes national security over the right to know. Attorney General Alberto Gonzales refused to provide a detailed explanation of how eavesdropping disrupted terrorist attempts because doing so would release important operational cues that could be used by terrorists. Although secrecy is not supposed to undermine "public deliberation and government accountability," skepticism toward government authority prompts public worry about threat inflation and over-classification. While it has been argued that democracy does not require unconditional publicity, Gutmann and Thompson argue that citizens should have a chance to decide whether a specific policy needs to be classified and whether the content of the policy should be subject to review after it is implemented.[22]

Debate on military secrecy should be concentrated not on whether the secrecy is legitimate or not, but rather on whether the secrecy is classified only for the purpose of furthering national security. The source of legitimacy therefore is whether the secrecy furthers citizens' interests, whether it furthers the right to know or the right to live in safety.

Rahul Sagar posits the invention of a regulatory framework that governs the classification process as the key factor in determining the legitimacy of a military secret. Lack of confidence and skepticism over governmental secrecy does not always stem from governmental abuse of power or over-classification, but from a malfunctioning of the framework resulting from disharmony in the self-discipline of the military in classifying secrets, legislative oversight, judicial arbitration and media investigation. More serious than the abuse of power and disharmony between watchdog organizations is the failure to understand that a regulatory framework with effective harmony is virtually impossible to create. One can hardly have 100 percent confidence that state secrecy will not be used to conceal governmental abuse of power.[23]

As unauthorized disclosure of classified information has become increasingly common, there is a tendency to regard it as morally justified civil disobedience against governmental abuse of power. Sagar further indicates that unauthorized disclosure can provide the most effective measure to prevent over-classification or misuse of secrecy. However, unauthorized leaks are also problematic. Unauthorized disclosure of classified information in the form of anonymous leaks may misguide public reaction. In addition, few leaks disclose behavior that can attract society-wide attention. In some cases, anonymous leaks are conducted to frame public reaction to further personal, bureaucratic or partisan interests. What is needed here is a definition of the source of the problem, whether threats to national security, over-classification of information by exaggerating the need for secrecy or ignorance of the people's right to know as it relates to national security. Unauthorized disclosure of military- and security-related information has become an increasingly common feature in South Korean society. Usually, unauthorized disclosure publicizes wrongdoing by government officials or excessive exercise of public authority. Doing so disperses government monopoly over classified information. However, in South Korea, unauthorized disclosure is regarded as an expression of distrust and civil disobedience against government authority that monopolizes access to secrets and controls the flow of information.[24]

On this, Sagar introduces two conservative viewpoints against unauthorized leaks. First, people who exercise government authority to manage the classification system are institutionally authorized by citizens because they are appointed by elected officials, whose job is to maintain balance between competing values and priorities. On the other hand, those involved in unauthorized disclosure, follow-up reporting and publishing of leaked information are "neither elected by the people nor appointed by their representatives." Second, there are institutional procedures and authorities such as elections and courts that collectively determine what is in the interest of national security. Individual and private judgments about what constitutes national security interests are not supposed to undermine these constitutional authorities and procedures. In addition, the anonymity that accompanies unauthorized disclosures could be used to cover up bureaucratic infighting.[25]

# 2

# The National Assembly in the Debate Between Civil Rights and National Security

Right after the shelling of Yeonpyeong Island in November 2011, a high-ranking government official, speaking on the condition of anonymity, worried about unauthorized leakage of highly sensitive military secrets during sessions of the National Assembly Committee of National Intelligence. During the sessions, discussions were held on South Korea's intelligence-gathering capability after the sinking of ROKS *Cheonan*, which resulted in the leakage of some procedures related to intelligence gathering. This was shared by the members of the Intelligence Committee and delivered to the public without redaction through interviews with the media. Based on the information, North Korea allegedly used telephone lines in the shelling of Yeonpyeong Island to avoid having its military communications intercepted by South Korea. The National Security Agency reportedly requested the National Assembly to stop unauthorized leaks to block the unwanted flow of sensitive military secrets to North Korea.

In this part of the book, an exploration of how the National Assembly performs its legal responsibility to oversee national security is in order. The government or the president might misuse control of classified secrets to disarm opposition leaders in the National

Assembly and citizen activist groups by limiting the scope of information to be released and by manipulating the timing of the release. It is very difficult to conclude whether state secrecy is used to conceal wrongdoing of government authority. Rather, Sagar posits that the focus should be on how to develop an institutional mechanism to empower members of the National Assembly.[1]

## Watchdogs or Undisciplined Leakers

There are contrasting views on the parliamentary handling of sensitive military secrets. The National Assembly, through its audit and oversight capability bestowed by the Constitution, serves as a watchdog against excessive use of secrecy. Those who criticize the National Assembly regard its members as amateurs and undisciplined leakers. First, the critics note its composition of adversarial parties that compete for political supremacy and use military secrecy as a political and campaign tool. Second, assembly members prioritize reelection over national security. Disclosure of sensitive information may help in an election by providing media exposure and thereby increasing their chances of being reelected. Third, high turnover at the Intelligence Committee, the obscurity of security issues and the lack of influence on member constituencies provide little incentive for developing expertise in the field. Officially, classified information should be released to assembly members for review in return for an official pledge of nondisclosure. Usually, the transfer of classified information may be made unofficially in return for a personal promise of nondisclosure. Antonin Scalia, assistant attorney general during the Ford administration, proposed the informal transfer of classified information to Congress in return for a promise of nondisclosure, which ultimately protected the president's control of state secrecy. Congressional investigation was launched only after high-profile cases drew media attention to governmental wrongdoings. The Church and Pike Committees in 1975, the Iran-Contra Committee in 1986, and the 9/11 Commission in 2003 were all launched after the media forced lawmakers to compel the government to release classified information.[2]

In the United States, it is not difficult to find cases in which members of Congress have challenged the intelligence services through deliberate leaks.[3] For example, Senator Burton Wheeler, who opposed U.S. entry into the Second World War, deliberately revealed government plans to send troops to Iceland in December 1941. His disclosure could have endangered American vessels with soldiers on board on their way to Europe when German submarines were aggressively attacking vessels carrying war-related materials. Secretary of War Henry Stimson accused Wheeler of action "that comes very near the lines of subversive activities against the United States, if not treason." Wheeler justified his disclosure as an exercise of his constitutional rights and added, "I shall continue to do everything in my power to keep Mr. Stimson from sending our boys to the bloody battlefields of Europe, Africa and Asia."[4] However, when Japan attacked Pearl Harbor a few days later, Wheeler himself supported the declaration of war against Japan.

Another widely cited example took place in 1974. Representative Michael Harrington released the content of sworn secret testimony by William Colby, then director of Central Intelligence, about U.S. efforts to overthrow President Salvador Allende of Chile. Right after Mr. Colby's testimony, Harrington twice read the testimony, which was kept in the subcommittee safe. Harrington then questioned the subcommittee chairman, Lucien Nedzi, who was later blamed by Harrington for ignoring illegal activities by the CIA. The *New York Times* reported on September 8 that the CIA was authorized to use more than $8 million to help keep Allende in power. What Harrington proposed to do was to challenge the classification of information on the part of those charged with the responsibility of making it classified. Though Harrington had initially agreed to keep Colby's testimony at the Intelligence Subcommittee confidential by signing a secrecy pledge, he later justified his decision to leak the information as part of "a greater duty" and mentioned that "signing a secrecy pledge does not excuse a Congressman or any other citizen from reporting evidence of a crime. Ordinarily, those who sign such agreements expect to see references to secret but legal activities." He added, "(the) enforcement of such an agreement to keep illegal activities secret is itself illegal." Harrington was convinced he was doing the right thing, saying, "I hope someday every American schoolchild will read that testimony."[5]

When a specific committee is headed by opposition party members, it is also probable that highly sensitive secrets may be misused for political purposes. In 1987, Les Aspin, a Wisconsin Democrat, then House Armed Services Committee chairman, leaked the exact dates of a military escort plan for Kuwaiti oil tankers in the Persian Gulf. Aspin, in opposition to the escort plan, told reporters that a Kuwaiti oil tanker flying the American flag would sail into the Persian Gulf under American military escort on July 22, followed by another on August 6. Disclosure of the exact dates of escort operations was sensitive because Defense Secretary Caspar Weinberger had not mentioned exact dates when asked about the operation. Aspin was criticized by Reagan administration officials for disclosing classified information. Aspin argued that he was not asked to keep the dates quiet and that he was not the only member who disclosed the exact dates.[6] The Rumsfeld Commission in 1998 accused the Clinton administration of forcing the CIA to downplay threats posed by ballistic missiles from North Korea and Iran, as a way to drive the country to pursue a national missile defense system.[7]

Deliberate leaks on Capitol Hill have been a traditional practice, and not a few have indicated that there are too many members in Congress and on committees to keep sensitive information secret. On October 1, 1776, Benjamin Franklin and Robert Morris, then members of the Committee of Secret Correspondence, did not share with other members of Congress an intelligence report that the French were willing to provide military aid. They justified their decision by arguing that "Congress consists of too many members to keep secrets." They later confessed that this realization arose from "fatal experiences" in the past. "Leaks were epidemic" in Congress, said Edward Boland, then chairman of the House Intelligence Committee, when Representative Clement Zablocki, the chairman of the House Foreign Affairs Committee, leaked information about covert operations against Libya to *Newsweek* in 1981. Zablocki, along with other members, had written to President Reagan to urge him to kill the operation plan.[8] The CIA secret operation, code-named "Canadian Caper" and designed to rescue American diplomats hiding in the Canadian Embassy in Tehran in 1979, was shared with Congress. The Carter administration informed Congress only after the three-month-long operation was completed because the Canadian government had promised its cooperation on the condition of keeping Congress in the dark about the operation. In so doing, President Jimmy Carter broke the law that required more timely notification of Congress.[9]

Things have changed since 9/11. Just 45 days after 9/11, Congress passed the USA Patriot Act on October 25, 2001, thereby allowing law enforcement authorities the power "to obtain sensitive private information about people, eavesdrop on conversations, monitor computer use, and detain suspects without probable cause." Patriot Act II authorized domestic wiretapping without a court order and access to financial records without subpoena.[10] Members of Congress mostly became "mute spectators" even when they acquired access to secret information because they were not allowed to discuss secrets with their staff, other experts and indeed fellow members who are not given access. Senator Jay Rockefeller had no choice but to convey his complaints privately to Vice President Cheney when he discovered NSA's warrantless wiretapping program after being briefed in his capacity as the vice chairman of the Senate Select Committee on Intelligence.[11] Other criticisms have labeled lawmakers as "uncritical cheerleaders." Rather than functioning as watchdogs over the government's handling of secrecy, they serve as silent justifiers of all claims the government makes for preserving national security. The most exemplary case has been the Joint Resolution on the Authorization for Use of Military Force against Terrorists, which authorized the president to use "all necessary and appropriate force against those nations, organizations, or persons" who "planned, authorized, committed, or aided terrorist attacks" on September 11.[12]

# The National Assembly and National Security Issues

The National Assembly is the most authoritative watchdog in Korea against governmental abuse of bureaucratic authority, including excessive classification and misuse of secrets. The National Assembly is able to deliver formal requests for testimony by heads of governmental departments and intelligence agencies, for attendance of officials in charge, and for disclosure of specific information. It can also pose an administrative burden by obstructing various confirmation processes for governmental appointees, by ratification of treaties and, most importantly, through the audit and review of budgets.[13]

South Korea's top intelligence organization, the National Intelligence Service, is stipulated by law to allow the National Assembly to access any and all classified information if the request satisfies procedural requirements also stipulated by law. The National Assembly possesses rare authority to access specific classified information. The National Intelligence Service Law allows the director of the agency to refuse submission of relevant materials or verbal testimony on matters that exert significant influence on national security. In case the director is requested by the Intelligence Committee of the National Assembly to submit materials, testify or answer a specific question, he may refuse to do so but must provide reasons why doing so would jeopardize national security. Then, the committee can ask the prime minister for further explanation, and if the prime minister fails to comply in seven days, the director must honor the committee's request.[14] The purpose of the law is to provide the National Assembly the necessary authority to perform its role as the watchdog of the government's handling of secrets.

In South Korea, its monopoly of classified information provides the government with very useful leverage to manipulate media attention and public opinion. When the NIS prediction that Kim Jong-un would pay a congratulatory visit to Russia proved wrong,[15] the NIS then released intelligence information to the National Assembly alleging that Hyun Young-ch'ol, North Korea's defense minister, had been executed. Two members of the Intelligence Committee publicized the information to the media, which made it a top story in South Korea.[16] In so doing, the NIS drove media attention away from its release of misinformation and shifted the spotlight over to the brutal execution of Hyun. The absolute monopoly over classified information held by the government makes it difficult for the National Assembly members to ascertain the real motives behind the release of classified information, which increases vulnerability to manipulation by the government and intelligence agencies.

Leaks by politicians, by citizen activists and sometimes by North Korea can manipulate the reactions of members of the National Assembly. Secrecy privileges for intelligence agencies are based on the notions of professional capability and constitutional responsibility to promote stability and security. The privilege is given to agencies and the government because the agents are professionally trained specialists who know how to act with secrecy and speed. The privilege is justified even when the government withholds classified information from requests made by the National Assembly. Unlike government branches and intelligence agencies which are composed of officials who owe their positions to the executive leadership of the president, making it less likely for them to release intelligence information against the president's will, the parliamentary committee is composed of adversarial party members who have greater incentives to disclose sensitive secrets for political advantage.[17]

What is unique in South Korea's parliament, the National Assembly, is the ratio of members who used to be journalists. Since 2000, ex-journalists have occupied 14 to 16 percent of all assembly seats. The ratio was higher in the 1990s, at more than 20 percent. Moreover, the number of ex-journalists on the committee in charge of the media has ranged from 25 percent to 44 percent, as shown in the table below.

| | 2000 | '02 | '04 | '06 | '08 | '10 | '12 | '14 | 2016 |
|---|---|---|---|---|---|---|---|---|---|
| Ex-journalists in the assembly | 16 | 16 | 14 | 14 | 14 | 14 | 10 | 10 | 8 |
| Ex-journalists on the Media Committee | 36 | 44 | 39 | 29 | 44 | 25 | 30 | 8 | 20 |

*Table 2–1: Committee on Culture & Tourism (2000–2008); Committee on Culture, Sports, Tourism, Broadcasting & Communications (2008–2012); Future Planning, Science, Broadcasting and Communication Committee (2012–present).*

In October 2004, the National Assembly issued warnings to then–opposition party members Park Jin and Chong Mun-hon for leaking military secrets. During a National Assembly audit of the Ministry of Defense, Park Jin disclosed the worst-case scenario of a North Korean invasion on the South by mentioning that North Korea could occupy Seoul within 16 days.[18] The ruling party members criticized Park for breaking Article 14 of the Law for National Audits and Investigations. Park's statement also ignited a debate on whether parliamentary immunity could allow assembly members to leak military secrets that would endanger national security. The National Security Agency launched an internal investigation into the Ministry of Unification for identifying paths through which the classified contingency plan was leaked to the National Assembly via the ministry. At the press conference, Park explained that he had acquired the information from the Korea Institute for Defense Analysis through legal means. He focused on the worst case, a simulated war-game result that hinted that the defense of Seoul would be impossible and that North Korean artillery would be fatally detrimental to the defense of the capital. Park concluded that his questions and statements during the audit had not released military secrets because no information was leaked to endanger national defense or national defense plans. He further explained that he did not quote from classified documents any sensitive information such as detailed data, strategic considerations, planned military deployments, or operation plans.

National Assembly opposition member Suh Nam-pyo once mentioned that North Korea did not have to send spies to South Korea due to the excessive release of military information in the media. Classified information may also be released during briefing sessions on military affairs at assembly hearings, which disclose highly sensitive information on arms deployment in the battlefield. On November 30, 2010, Defense Minister Kim Tae-young's testimony disclosed classified plans to deploy the Pegasus land-to-air missile system onto the island of Yeonpyeong.[19] In addition, Kim Hak-song, then chairman of the Defense Committee of the South Korean National Assembly, released the content of a classified briefing by the Ministry of Defense stating that the South Korean military had failed to track one of the two North Korean submarines operating in the West Sea on the day of the sinking of the ROKS *Cheonan* while the other was detected as communicating with a naval base. This classified information disclosed to North Korea the weaknesses of submarine detection capacity. Conservative media outlets like the *Chosun Ilbo* warned the leakers about making sensitive military information public, while liberal media such as the *Kyunghyang Shinmun* complained about excessive redaction when the South Korean military refused to release the contents of communication records between the ROKS *Cheonan* and a naval base.[20]

Members of the National Assembly sometimes deliberately engage in unauthorized disclosure of secrets in order to cripple a policy or to stop implementation of the policy. This kind of unauthorized disclosure takes place when a policy cannot be defeated through a normal decision making process.[21] In August 2006, Lee Sung-ku, a ruling party member of the National Defense Committee at the National Assembly, provided the media with a document containing information on anti-artillery measures of the U.S. forces in Korea including military satellites and reconnaissance planes, as well as the anti-artillery capability of the South Korean army. The document was provided during the Ulchi Focus Lens exercise to the members of the National Assembly Committee for National Defense on the condition of secrecy. During a press briefing on March 26, 2010, the spokesperson for the Ministry of Defense registered his regret regarding irresponsible and unauthorized disclosure of military secrets surrounding the sinking of the ROKS *Cheonan*. He added that the maintenance of military secrecy was a critical requirement not only for the success of military operations but for protecting the lives of soldiers in emergencies. This statement came ten days after the sinking of the ROKS *Cheonan* due to unauthorized leaks of highly classified sensitive information on the operational routes of North Korean submarines, as acquired from reconnaissance flights by U-2 reconnaissance planes, from satellite imagery and mostly by tapping North Korean communication frequency channels. Leaks of information acquired from frequency tapping led North Korea to change the frequency it used, which necessitated the investment of much effort and time in searching for the new frequency. Kim Hak-song, chairman of the National Defense Committee of the National Assembly, mentioned on April 5 that communication by a North Korean submarine was detected, which, according to the South Korean military, caused North Korea's change of frequency. Tracking the new frequency would take several months, during which the whereabouts of North Korean submarines could not be detected. The military launched an internal investigation to verify the content of military secrets submitted to the National Assembly.

The sinking of ROKS *Cheonan* ignited a hot debate about

military secrecy and the right to know. The sinking was the first incident of its kind, in which a 1,200-ton military vessel was torn into two parts, drawing nationwide attention and triggering increased calls for the right to know. The navy publicized an 80-second-long edited version of a TOD (thermal observation device) visual record, which generated doubts about intentional concealment of the truth. The navy later publicized an unedited version of a 40-minute-long record to clear up unnecessary suspicions. As a result of a request from the families of crew members for disclosure of communication records between the ROKS *Cheonan* and the nearby ROKS *Sokcho*, the navy stated that disclosure of communication records was impossible because even the edited version contained highly sensitive information about ongoing military operations. The navy further explained that the communication records themselves were classified.

Defense Minister Kim Tae-young, at a general session of the National Assembly, disclosed that intelligence agencies regularly looked at North Korea's submarine bases through satellite observation. He also mentioned that two North Korean submarines were out of observation on the day of the ROKS *Cheonan* sinking, which may have given North Korea hints about blind points in the observation program as well as the frequency of satellite observation. Roughly six months later, assembly member Shin Hak-yong, during his interview with a major TV news program, disclosed that the navy had not made proper preparations even after detecting the unscheduled operation of a North Korean submarine on the day of the ROKS *Cheonan* sinking. The Defense Security Command, a military intelligence organization, mentioned its plan to investigate Shin for unauthorized public leakage of military secrets. The military argued that Shin's disclosure revealed not only the content of a Military Secret III but also South Korea's intelligence-gathering capabilities, along with its decoding system. Shin argued that his disclosure was in accordance with his constitutional duty to oversee flawed security posture and to find measures to remedy system flaws.

## 2. The National Assembly, Civil Rights and National Security

What is lacking in the National Assembly is not the professional capability of members to handle sensitive military secrets. Most members in the Intelligence Committee are retired military generals or high-ranking officials in intelligence agencies and have been National Assembly members for several terms. What is lacking is public trust in the National Assembly and in the professional capabilities of intelligence agencies.

# 3

# The Courts and National Security

## Legal Judgments Regarding Civil Rights and National Security

### The Definition of Military Secrets in South Korea

Since 2010, seventeen cases involving 34 persons have been reported for breaking the Military Secret Protection Law, with only one suspect convicted and sentenced to prison and remanded into custody. In addition, 7,116 army soldiers, 3,364 navy sailors and 403 air force soldiers received official warnings for breaking military secrecy. The number of cases has increased year by year. Some 1,981 soldiers were charged for leaking secrets in 2010, 2,311 in 2011, 2,692 in 2012, and 2,650 in 2013. Increased numbers of leaks were witnessed in the army, from 1,444 in 2010 to 1,480 in 2011 to 1,551 in 2012 to 1,779 in 2013. This was disclosed by Lee Han-sung, a ruling party assembly member.

How to define a military secret is a hotly debated issue in South Korea. Under authoritarian military rule before democratization in 1987, the definition of a military secret tended to represent a broader conceptualization which was justified by military confrontation with North Korea. Then the 1993 version of the Military Secret Protection Law incorporated a more specified redefinition of military secrets that included information that was not yet known to the public, as well as classified information. Article 2 of the Military Secret Protection Law defines a military secret as "a special media record or object such as military-related document, picture, electronic record, etc. that is not made known to the general public and, if leaked, could cause clear damage to national security, and is thus identified or listed as a military secret or properly protected as such."[1] The article broadly defines military secrets to include (1) information regarding military policy, strategy, diplomacy and military plans for operation and deployment, (2) military information regarding organization, equipment and mobilization, (3) information on military intelligence, (4) information on military transportation, (5) information on production, supply and development of military equipment, requisites and supplies, (6) personnel information on major departments in the military, and (7) information on organization, equipment and mobilization of reserve forces.

In South Korea, the definition of the scope of military secrecy is more important than whether to respect mosaic theory. In 1989, the Constitutional Court of Korea included "the right to know" into freedom of expression by ruling that "the formation of free will is possible only through guaranteeing access to sufficient information—access, collection and processing of information, that is, the right to know is undoubtedly a part of freedom of expression."[2] In 1992, the Constitutional Court of Korea made it clear that limiting civil liberty for national security should be permitted to a degree that does not infringe upon core rights. The ruling indicates that an excessively enlarged realm of military secrets that could be in conflict with civil rights might draw military affairs out of civilian control, and thus would be against the basic ideology of the Constitution.[3]

In the process of democratization, a redefinition of national secrecy was also introduced. A Supreme Court ruling in September 1997 defined national secrets as all political, economic, social and cultural facts, subjects and knowledge that would serve national interests only when they are kept secret or are not exposed to antigovernmental parties. At the same time, those facts, subjects and knowledge should bear actual value to be classified as military secrets only in cases where their disclosure endangers national security. The court also ruled that its definition did not include those facts, subjects or knowledge which were widely known to civilians, in accordance with legal procedures.[4]

In 2002, the Seoul High Court ruled that certain information cannot be disclosed even upon proper legal requests, in accordance with the Public Information Law. Information regarding military operation command systems, operational situations, decision-making procedures and the size, location and deployment of troops are off limits to requests for the disclosure of information, in accordance with the Public Information Law. In addition, information that could endanger civilian life in any way is off limits. Two years later, in September 2004, the ruling was confirmed by the Supreme Court.[5]

The year 1997 witnessed numerous court rulings that narrowed the realm of secrecy. In 1997, the District Court of Seoul ruled that providing brief information about the domestic context drawn from newspapers and journals did not constitute endangering national security.[6] It was in July 1997 that the Supreme Court, by reversing a High Court sentence, found pro–North Korean organization members who provided North Korea with tapes and investigation records about legal trials over antigovernment activities not guilty. The High Court had ruled that these pro–North Korean activists violated the National Security Law by collecting and delivering information on South Korea's domestic politics, antigovernment organizations, and trial records of members under direction from North Korea. The High Court added that, although the information was widely known and not collected in illegal ways, it could be defined as a national secret in broad terms if it could be of use to North Korea and also if Pyongyang's knowledge of the information could be detrimental to South Korea. Here, the High Court applied a broader definition of national secrets. The Supreme Court ruling acknowledged the defendants' appeal against a broader definition of national secrets as reasonable and sent the case back to the High Court. The ruling resulted in a thorough reevaluation of what was considered a national secret and what was not.[7]

It was also in 1997 that the Supreme Court reversed a High Court ruling by indicating that information about a local agricultural community did not belong to the realm of national secrets. The accused was charged with verbally delivering information about his local agricultural community to a North Korean agent whose identity, according to the Supreme Court judges, was not entirely exposed to the accused. The Supreme Court also noted a lack of evidence to support the charge that the accused intended to endanger national security or to be helpful to North Korea by providing information to the North Korean agent.[8]

In 1997, the Supreme Court ruled that personal information about long-term communist prisoners, the location of their prisons, life conditions in prison cells and prisoners' present ideological status could be regarded as military secrets. In addition, the Supreme Court handed down a guilty verdict in a case centered around providing North Korea with geographical information of areas along the DMZ and South Korea's attempts to search for North Korea's underground tunnels underneath South Korean soil. The Supreme Court indicated that the information was not widely known to the public and could feasibly endanger national security if leaked.[9]

There is no rational answer to the question of how much harm a specific disclosure causes to national security under a certain situation. What should be noted here is that the intelligence business is far from being a science with objective answers. It has been mentioned that "the business of intelligence is an inexact science at best."[10] In November 2003, the Supreme Court handed down a not-guilty verdict for a top-ranking NSA official who was charged with leaking ongoing internal inspections and thereby magnifying suspicions of the NSA's alleged wiretapping activity and ultimately obstructing the normal information-gathering activity of the NSA.

The accused in this case was the director of Internal Affairs at the NSA, who had been regional chief of the Gwangju region when he leaked the information about internal inspections, including the starting point of the inspection and personal information related to the targets of the investigation. The Supreme Court mentioned that the definition of a secret should be strictly limited in order to maximize freedom of expression and the right to know. The Supreme Court also indicated that secrets should be unknown facts that deserved to be protected. The Supreme Court clarified that the leaked information was hardly unknown to the public and did not have a direct influence on the NSA's normal operations. The Supreme Court concluded that the leaks could not harm the normal information-collecting activity of the NSA and did not endanger the function of the NSA. Thus, the Supreme Court ruled that the charge, in accordance with Article 17 of the Law on NSA Employees, should be dismissed.[11]

In 1997, the Supreme Court reversed the decision by the Seoul High Court that leaking information from newspapers and the media could constitute criminal activity, in accordance with the National Security Law. The accused was charged with conveying information acquired from a pamphlet distributed at an international defense industry exposition and through asking questions to experts at a lecture session of the Asia-Pacific Foundation, the chairman of which was the opposition leader Kim Dae-jung, who later became president of South Korea. The High Court of Seoul indicated that information acquired at events such as the defense industry exposition could not be regarded as widely known facts because those events were open only to a limited number of experts. In addition, the accused was charged for providing North Korea with information about South Korea's domestic politics, public opinion, foreign and military relations, and hosting of sports events during the period between 1984 and 1996. The Supreme Court acknowledged that the above-mentioned information could endanger national security if leaked to North Korea, and thereby belonged to the category of national secrets, as stipulated by the National Security Law, Article 4, Clause 1, Section 2 (na). However, with regard to other charges of leaking information acquired from open sources and information that was widely known to the public, the Supreme Court indicated there could be a misunderstanding of legal principles in defining national secrets in accordance with the National Security Law, which could have influenced the High Court's ruling. The Supreme Court further indicated that what information could be defined as national secrets when applying Article 4, Section 2, of Clause 1 should be distinguished. The Supreme Court sent the case to the High Court of Seoul to reconsider its sentence, based on mistaken application of the National Security Law in defining national secrets.[12]

In May 2002, the Supreme Court reversed the ruling by the High Court in April 2000 that had found the accused guilty for leaking information on SADARM bullets included in "the mid- and long-term military plan of 1998–2002," which was classified as a Military Secret II. The accused was a team leader in charge of supplying ammunition at the Ammunition Supplication Command when his civilian acquaintance picked up his report on the current status of ammunition allocation from his drawer. His acquaintance produced a report on the "SADARM bullet project," behavior that constituted the leaking of military secrets. In addition, the accused was charged with providing information on military plans for appropriate ammunition supply for the years of 2001, 2002 and 2003. The Supreme Court ruled that the leaked information, part of which was classified, could hardly be regarded as a military secret in accordance with the standard procedure for classifying a Military Secret II or a Military Secret III. Therefore, the Supreme Court found the defendant not guilty and sent the case to the High Court.[13]

A similar trend of limiting the sphere of secrecy is found in U.S. court rulings, especially several years after September 11. *Horn v. Huddle* (2009)[14] highlighted that procedural requirements in invoking state secret privileges should not be taken lightly. In this case, plaintiff Horn claimed that defendant Franklin Huddle, with the assistance of defendant Arthur Brown, unlawfully eavesdropped on Horn's private conversation by using the CIA's surveillance equipment in Rangoon, Burma, in 1992 and 1993, in violation of the Fourth Amendment. In 1992, Horn was working for the Drug Enforcement Agency while Huddle was an employee of the Department of State and Brown was a CIA agent. All three were involved in sensitive governmental activities in Rangoon. The court concluded that the case could not proceed due to the risks of revealing state secrets. In particular, the court concluded that no information about CIA agent Brown, including even his name, would be admissible at trial. Later, the court learned that the identity of Brown as the CIA agent was not covert as of 2002 and also discovered that Brown and the CIA perpetrated fraud targeting the court. District Judge Royce Lamberth of the District of Columbia penalized CIA officials and their lawyers for behavior including fraudulent invocation of state secret privileges. As a result, the CIA settled the case by reaching a $3 million settlement with the plaintiff. This case signaled to intelligence agencies that court judges were not to be fooled or trifled with.

## Is Already Published Information Still Secret?

In discussing the sphere of secrecy, whether information already publicized deserves secrecy protection attracts scholarly discussion. Mainstream views held by courts do not respect the secrecy of classified information which has already been made known to the public. In the United States, war protesters began to file suits against government intelligence agencies which they believed had intercepted their communications without warrant. *Halkin v. Helms* (1978)[15] was an exemplary case that showed that the secret privilege cannot be invoked when the relevant information has already been revealed in a congressional report. It was Adele Halkin, an antiwar protester, who brought this case to the court because it was believed that warrantless surveillance had taken place. Officials and former officials of the NSA, CIA, DIA, FBI and Secret Service were the defendants. When a request to identify individuals or organizations whose communications were intercepted was refused by the NSA, the case was filed. The issue in this case was whether the NSA should be ordered to disclose whether communications involving the plaintiff were acquired by the NSA and shared by other government agencies and whether admittance or denial of such acquisitions would damage national security by revealing the NSA's foreign intelligence collection capabilities.

The NSA argued that such disclosure would present a reasonable danger by enabling foreign intelligence agencies to "extrapolate" the focus and concern of the NSA. Accordingly, the court ruled that the plaintiffs' requests to release information regarding NSA's intercepts from operation MINARET should be turned down. However, at the same time, the court ruled that information about NSA's SHAMROCK intercept operation should be released to the plaintiffs because congressional report had already revealed much about the information, so national security would not be harmed by the disclosure of the existence of the intercepts. Both the plaintiffs and the NSA appealed. While upholding its former rule about the release of information that had already been disclosed by congressional examination, the court referred to the mosaic theory in confirming its deference to the secret privilege against disclosing intercepts from MINARET.

... (t)he standard of review for state secret privilege claims must be a narrow one. Judges must be cautious in challenging claims about the need to withhold information that might seem trivial or unimportant to ordinary observers. The business of foreign intelligence gathering in this age of computer technology is more akin to the construction of a mosaic because bits and pieces of seemingly innocuous information can be analyzed and fitted into place to reveal with startling clarity how the unseen whole must operate. The court must accord the utmost deference to executive assertions of privilege upon grounds of military or diplomatic secrets.[16]

*Mohamed v. Jeppesen Data Plan Inc.* (2009) and *Mohamed v. Jeppesen Data Plan Inc.* (2010)[17] demonstrated a line that can be drawn between judicial judgment and state power to invoke secret privileges. Jeppesen Data Plan Incorporated, a Boeing subsidiary, was accused of arranging flights for the CIA to transfer terrorist suspects to overseas secret detention facilities for imprisonment and interrogation. Binyam Mohamed, an Ethiopian citizen and legal resident of Britain, was allegedly arrested in Pakistan in 2002 and then turned over to the CIA. In October 2006, the *New Yorker* reported that the company had provided navigational and logistical support for the CIA, quoting comments made by former employees in anonymity. Then, Amnesty International demonstrated in front of the company's office in San Jose, California, and the American Civil Liberties Union (ACLU) sued the company on behalf of five former prisoners including Mohamed, who argued they had been tortured in captivity in CIA detention facilities in Morocco, Egypt and Afghanistan.

The CIA intervened before Mohamed's appeal reached the trial stage at the District Court of the Northern District of California by arguing that the majority of the plaintiffs' complaints were related to covert CIA operations. The court accepted the CIA's intervention as reasonable and dismissed the case in February 2008. Then, the plaintiffs filed an appeal to the United States Court of Appeals for the Ninth Circuit, which affirmed the dismissal of the suit in September 2010 in a 6–5 *en banc* ruling. The ACLU also filed an appeal with the Supreme Court, which in May 2011 declined to review the decision of the Ninth Circuit to dismiss the case, thereby drawing a line between judiciary jurisdiction and state secret privileges.

Before the Ninth Circuit dismissed the case, a three-judge panel on the Ninth Circuit adopted a narrower view of how to define state secrecy. In this, Judge Michael Hawkins ruled against the notion that a lawsuit should be dismissed whenever a complaint contained allegations which included parts classified as secret. He observed that the judiciary was not supposed to immunize secret operations of the CIA and other government agencies by cordoning them off from judicial scrutiny. When the constitutional separation of administrative power and judicial jurisdiction was questioned, he argued, an "item-by-item" analysis was required to tell whether the invoked evidence was "genuinely indispensable" for maintaining the suit or whether it was possible to continue the case by referring to non-privileged evidence. Judge Hawkins went on to the issue of what counted as a state secret by questioning whether a classified matter could be equated with a state secret. Because unquestioned equation of classified issues with state secrets would encourage the president to classify all politically embarrassing information to cordon it off from judicial review, the court should engage in an independent judicial process to determine whether an invoked secret constituted a secret within the legal meaning of the secret privilege. Judge Hawkins, after his own evaluation of the evidence, concluded that classified information published in the *Pentagon Papers* and then re-reported by the *New York Times* could not be claimed as secret even when the government refused to declassify it.

Then, the Obama administration appealed to the entire San Francisco–based appeals court, where a group of 11 judges voted to rehear the case *en banc* and ruled in favor of the CIA's claim of secret privilege by affirming the former decision made by the California district court by a margin of 6–5. According to Judge Raymond Fisher, who wrote for the majority, the Ninth Circuit ruled that disclosure of the existence of extraordinary rendition programs should not preclude other relevant information from remaining state secrets if disclosure would harm national security. However, the ruling did acknowledge that the existence of a rendition program which had been already published in newspapers could not be regarded as a state secret.

The South Korean courts demonstrate case-by-case judgment over classified secrets which have already been made public. In 1994, the Supreme Court acknowledged the Military High Court's ruling that photocopies of material classified as a Military Secret

III, the content of which was introduced in foreign military journals and disclosed to domestic institutions specializing in security affairs, still belonged in the category of military secrets. The Supreme Court acknowledged that military secrets, although disclosed somewhere else, maintained their validity as effective military secrets as long as they remained classified.[18]

In September 2006, the High Court of Daejeon ruled that detailed information on search radar, including its maximum search range, search degree and capacity, which was classified as a Military Secret III, should not be disclosed to the public even though the information was widely shared by radar experts. The High Court also ruled that the information contained sensitive data used to predict South Korea's future military posture and military capacity, which could ultimately endanger national security.[19]

However, in December 2007, the Supreme Court handed down a not-guilty verdict for behavior involving the negligent release of military information on the IPT project and third-class military secrets, including the "Mid-Term Military Plan of 2006~2010," which had already been made public. The rule was based on the following judgment: First, the IPT project was not classified; second, military secrets that had already been made public could not be acknowledged to be classified information; third, the information had gone through a sufficient secret screening process before publication; fourth, the information released on the IPT project did not include information on the entire project; and last, most experts on the IPT project did not consider the information as classified or secret.

Also in October 2011, the Supreme Court ruled that uploading sensitive military information was not a violation of the National Security Law if the uploaded information was already publicized on the internet. Again, lack of intention to harm national security or to be of help to North Korea was an important factor used to determine whether uploading photographs of military facilities and airfields was a crime that violated the National Security Law.

## Acceptance of the Mosaic Theory

The court faces the challenge of choosing between military secrecy and civil rights. It is unsure whether it is possible to measure and weigh between "the government's need to conceal, the media's need to publish and the people's need to know." There is no firm basis to compare competing interests that are unobjectionable in general. The court faces the difficulty of judging whether a specific disclosure of secrecy is harmful to national security and at the same time important for civil rights. If the disclosure is harmful, the court must estimate the degree of harm caused to national security.[20] In cases of unauthorized disclosures when disclosed information has already been published elsewhere, measuring harm caused to national security and benefits in expanding civil rights may be very difficult.

Choosing whether to acknowledge the validity of the mosaic theory propositions is critical in determining whether to respect secrecy, its scope and the secret privilege of government. Mosaic theory posits that a piece of information that seems to be meaningless by itself may contain valuable and sensitive information that can harm national security if aggregated. Information about a casual tea-time gathering of wives of North Korea elites may be classified not because the gathering itself or the conversation there is important but because the source the information was collected from needs to be protected.

In the United States, it is not difficult to find cases where court rules respect mosaic theory. *Fitzgibbon v. CIA*[21] was an exemplary case in which the court trusted the assessment of the CIA over whether the release of specific information would be harmful to national security. In particular, the CIA argued that the release of requested documents would reveal fractured information about the CIA's relations with foreign intelligence agencies, locations of CIA stations, sources of information, and methods of investigation. Alan Fitzgibbon, a historian, asked the CIA to provide information with regard to the disappearance and assumed death in 1956 of Jesus de Galindez, a critic of the Dominican Rafael Trujillo regime. He lived in New York City and taught at Columbia University before his disappearance. The Trujillo regime was anticommunist and at the same time was notorious for its repressive rule. Galindez was allegedly executed with the unwitting aid of American pilot Gerald Murphy, whose body was found in the Dominican Republic. The CIA provided only 21 out of 551 documents relating to the Galindez affair. Dissatisfied with the documents released by the CIA, which contained heavy redactions, Fitzgibbon brought the case to the District Court for the District of Columbia in 1979. The CIA justified its decision to withhold the information by filing a classified affidavit. After examining the original content of the deleted part of the documents *in camera*, District Judge Harold Greene ordered the disclosure of the redacted parts of the documents. According to Judge Greene's description, the documents were "so basic and innocent" that their release would not harm national security. The CIA appealed the decision. On remand, Judge Greene reversed his previous order. However, he insisted on the disclosure of redacted parts that identified the location of a CIA station because the location had already been disclosed by a congressional report. This decision was appealed by both the CIA and Fitzgibbon. The CIA tried to reverse the order to disclose information regarding the location of its station, while Fitzgibbon argued for full disclosure of the documents in accordance with the previous court order. The District of Columbia Circuit Court rejected Fitzgibbon's appeal. More important was Judge David Sentelle's statement that "the assessment of harm to intelligence sources, methods and operations is entrusted to the Director of Central Intelligence, not to the courts." Despite investigations by the New York Police Department, the FBI and the CIA, separately and jointly, the disappearance of Galindez and the role of Murphy remain a public mystery.

In *Gardels v. CIA* (1982),[22] officials did offer affidavits in public for explaining why confirming or denying the existence of the state secret in question could harm national security, although they maintained the stance of non-circumvention non-disclosure (NCND) over the existence of the secret. In this case, the existence of covert CIA contacts with the UC Berkeley community was in question. Nathan Gardels, then a student at UCLA, sought disclosure by the CIA under the Freedom of Information Act (FOIA) of past and present contacts between the CIA and 11 University of California campuses. Although the CIA provided documents relating to overt contacts, it told Gardels that the agency "would neither confirm nor deny the existence of any documents revealing covert CIA connections or interests with the University." Then, Gardels brought the case to the district court under the FOIA, and the CIA filed a motion for summary judgment, which was granted by the court on the basis of Exemption 3 of the FOIA. The CIA explained that identifying universities where it had no covert contacts would lead foreign intelligence organizations to target remaining universities for the purpose of discovering CIA contacts, and that therefore it should take an NCND position. This explanation is understandable; however, the CIA did not provide any evidence of how its contacts were managed properly or how acknowledging such contacts would harm national security.

One stark difference in defining military secrets in South Korea is that the court does not always respect mosaic theory. In 1990, the Supreme Court ruled that the location and designation/cancellation of military restricted areas belonged to the category of military secrets. In this case, the accused was charged with spreading rumors that restrictions over several military areas would be terminated. The accused referred to campaign slogans of the presidential and parliamentary elections that military areas around Seoul would no longer be designated as such. The court ruled that military restricted areas were designated for the protection of military facilities and the facilitation of military operations, and that the designation and cancellation of such designation were thereby essential military secrets. The court added that designation/cancellation of military restricted areas belonged to the category of military secrets in accordance with Article 80 of the Military Criminal Law because the designation/termination of military restricted areas was conducted by the Military Operation Bureau of the Joint Chiefs of Staff in a manner commensurate with classified-level operations.[23]

## Civilian Requests for Access to Classified Information

What requires further discussion is whether to respect civilian requests to disclose classified information processed through legal procedure. In South Korea, the people's right to know and freedom of expression are civil liberties guaranteed by the Constitution. To protect those constitutional rights, Article 3 of the Public Information Law stipulates all information should in principle be released to the public when legally requested unless it belongs to the category of classified information stipulated by Article 7–1. Even in this case, one has to review and ascertain whether there exist any conflicts of interest or rights or any reasonable grounds as to why certain information should not be publicized.

*United States v. Reynolds* (1953)[24] is an exemplary case in which the court defended the government's secret privilege. The case was filed by widows of three employees of the Radio Corporation of America, an air force contractor. The employees were killed when a B-29 bomber crashed in 1948 in Waycross, Georgia, during a secret mission for testing electronic equipment. The widows brought a tort action seeking damages under the Federal Tort Claims Act, and as part of this action, they requested access to the accident report over the crash. The air force refused to release detailed information by citing the right to withhold secret documents for national security. The plaintiffs filed a suit against the air force for its negligence, and the district court treated the claim of negligence as justified and forced the air force to award damages.

A directed verdict in favor of the plaintiffs was granted by the trial court. Then the United States appealed, and the appeal went all the way to the Supreme Court after the directed verdict was affirmed by the United States Court of Appeals for the Third Circuit. The Supreme Court reversed the decision and remanded it to the trial court by a 6–3 ruling, stating that "even the most compelling necessity" of the plaintiff "cannot overcome the claim of privilege if the court is ultimately satisfied that military secrets are at stake."

In this case, the court tried to reach a balance between judicial control and administrative privilege for national security. Too much emphasis on judicial control would force the administration to release sensitive information its privilege was designed to protect, while complete abandonment of judicial control would generate civil liberty abuses through misuse of administrative privileges. The court took a compromised stance by stating that judicial control over the evidence "cannot be abdicated to the caprice of executive officers," while affirming that the court would not overrule the claim of privilege by requesting complete and automatic submission of evidence to the court. The chief justice mentioned that executive privilege over evidence was appropriate in the case, since disclosure would jeopardize national security. The court ruled that the accident investigation report was privileged, due to the reasonable danger to sensitive secrets regarding electronic equipment the crashed airplane had attempted to test. The court ruling in the *United States v. Reynolds* (1953) case could have triggered scholarly debate on whether authorized release of the accident report would have harmed national security.

Declassification of the accident report led to refiled litigation of the case as *Herring v. United States* (2003) in the United States District Court for the Eastern District of Pennsylvania. The accident report, declassified in 2000, indicated the B-29 crashed due to a fire in one of its engines. The document also indicated a settlement was reached after the Supreme Court ruling and that the widows received an aggregate sum of $170,000 in exchange for a release of government liability as of June 1953. The radio program *This American Life* reported that the accident report contained no information on the secret equipment except that the equipment was present on the plane. The program interviewed the daughter of one of the victims, who argued that the government's claims in the case were fraudulent. The new litigation attempted to overturn the Supreme Court ruling for a writ of error *coram nobis*, based on the claim that the use of the "secret" label constituted defrauding the court. The trial court found no fraud in the government's claim of secret privilege in 1953, which was upheld by the Court of Appeals for the Third Circuit. The court ruling indicated that information about the mission by an aircraft capable of dropping bombs at altitudes of 20,000 feet and above could have been "seemingly insignificant pieces of information" that "would have been of keen interest to a Soviet spy fifty years ago."

*Ellsberg v. Mitchell* (1983)[25] was another case where the government defended its position against requests for more public and open invocation of state secret privileges. In this case, Daniel Ellsberg and his attorneys, who were defendants of the Pentagon Papers case, sought compensation for damages after learning they had been subjected to unwarranted electronic surveillance. They submitted testimony from each of the defendants and learned that Ellsberg's conversations were accidentally overheard. The defendants refused to respond on the grounds that all relevant information was privileged. Their refusal was buttressed by formal claims of privilege by then–Attorney General Richard Kleindienst, who submitted records of intercepted conversations, including locations and identity, in a sealed exhibit to the district court for an *in camera* inspection. When the District Court for the District of Columbia ruled in support of government invocation of state secret privileges, the plaintiffs approached the D.C. Circuit. The affidavits submitted by the government failed to specify the interests and how those interests would be damaged by disclosing the requested information. Judge Harry Edwards stated that public submission of affidavits could not be strictly enforced because the procedure to evaluate the legitimacy of the state invocation was not supposed to endanger the very thing secret privilege was designed to protect. He added, "the more specific the public explanation, the greater the ability of the opposing party to contest it."

In *Kasza v. Browner* (1998),[26] the Ninth Court also ruled in favor of secret privilege invoked by the air force. Former workers once hired by the air force wanted disclosure of unlawful handling of hazardous waste at a secret air force base in Nevada. The plaintiffs alleged that the air force unlawfully handled hazardous waste, thereby violating the Resource Conservation and Recovery Act in a classified place in Nevada. The air force invoked the state secrets privilege by refusing to confirm or deny whether hazardous materials were generated, stored or disposed at the base. The district court dismissed the case, and the plaintiffs brought the case to the Ninth Circuit by arguing that the existence of hazardous materials could not be a secret. The Ninth Circuit Court acknowledged, after *in camera* review, that disclosure of even unclassified information about the material could expose sensitive parts of classified secrets and dismissed the entire action. The Ninth Circuit concluded that the "very subject matter of action is a state secret."

*Weatherhead v. U.S.* (1998)[27] was a case in which Leslie Weatherhead sent identical requests to the Justice Department and State Department for a copy of the letter from the British Foreign Office to George Proctor, director of the Office of International Affairs at the Justice Department. The letter was about the extradition of two British citizens, Sally Croft and Susan Hagan, from the United Kingdom to the United States to stand trial for the murder of the U.S. attorney for Oregon. The State Department replied that it had been unable to locate the letter, which was followed two weeks later by the reply from the Justice Department that it had found the letter. The Justice Department added that the document was produced by a foreign government, which required the department to consult with the State Department. The State Department inquired whether the British government wanted any portion of the letter to be withheld, and the British government replied that it was unable to agree to the release of the letter.

After consulting with the British government and concluding that the correspondence was confidential, the State Department rejected Weatherhead's requests under FOIA Exemption 1, which prompted him to bring the case to the District Court for the Eastern District of Washington. At first, the court ordered the letter to be disclosed because it failed to find the government's affidavits justifying the withholding of correspondence. After an appeal for reconsideration, however, Judge Frederick Van Sickle conducted an *in camera* review, which led him to reverse his earlier decision to withhold the correspondence because he found that no portion of the letter could be disclosed without simultaneously disclosing sensitive material.

Now, the plaintiff appealed to the Ninth Circuit, which concluded the opposite after conducting an *in camera* review and ordered the release of the letter. Chief Judge Procter Hug wrote for the majority, "we fail to comprehend how disclosing the letter at this time could cause harm to the national defense or foreign relations of the United States. The letter is innocuous." "(W)e judges are outside of our area of expertise here," wrote Judge Barry Silverman for the minority, who argued that the examination of the existence of facts was different from the evaluation of the sensitivity of classified documents and the damage that disclosure of such documents would cause to national security.

What was ironic was that the British consul in Seattle had sent a significant portion of the letter to the plaintiff long before the court decision was reached, and the plaintiff had no reason to proceed further. Dissatisfied with the Ninth Circuit decision, the U.S. government appealed to the Supreme Court when the litigants discovered the delivery of the letter by the British consul. Subsequently, no further litigation continued.

*Jabara v. Kelley* (1977) was a case in which the court partially supported the claim of a plaintiff who had been subjected to warrantless wiretapping. When refused access to information regarding the wiretapping, the plaintiff sought assistance from the District Court of the Eastern District of Michigan, while the Department of Defense invoked the state secret privilege claim for all information that might reveal foreign intelligence sources and capabilities. At the same time, however, the judge ruled that the privilege could not be invoked to shield information not directly relevant to the conduct of foreign intelligence, such as the name of a federal agency, the NSA in this case, because its name had already been revealed in a congressional report. He added that "it would be a farce" to regard the name of the agency as a military secret. In *Hepting v. AT&T* (2006) and *ACLU v. NSA* (2006), the courts found an interesting precedent of compelling an intelligence agency to officially acknowledge the existence of a warrantless surveillance program. Confronted with state invocations of secret privilege by the NSA that prevented the plaintiffs from accessing any information to prove that they had been subject to warrantless wiretaps, the courts concluded that the NSA's official acknowledgment of the existence of the wiretapping program without warrant was sufficient. In doing so, the courts could allow the plaintiffs to proceed with their cases while opening a way for NSA officials to say as little as possible without disclosing any details in public.[28]

In 1996, the National Security Planning Agency (now the NSA) in Korea was asked to publicize the process of producing, using, distributing and storing videotapes about antigovernment organizations. When the NSPA refused to do so, the plaintiff filed a suit against it. The plaintiff, by invoking the Public Information Act, requested the videotaped material produced by the Research Institute for Inter–Korean Relations, a branch organization of the NSPA, and the briefing slides used at the NPSA's briefing session for judicial apprentices. The plaintiff also requested that the financial budget used to produce, use, distribute and store the materials be made public. The NPSA acknowledged that some parts of the videotape content caused misunderstandings while refusing to publicize the materials because the videotapes were abandoned and the slides were classified. The plaintiff argued that the NPSA's decision was against a citizen's right to know, guaranteed by the Constitution, while the NPSA argued that a citizen's right to know may be limited for national security, maintenance of order and public welfare, in accordance with the second clause of Article 37 of the Constitution and also in accordance with the NSPA Law and the NSPA Employee Law. The Seoul High Court in November 1997 accepted NSPA's argument that a citizen's right to know may be limited by the Constitution and that public information could also be kept secret when it conflicted with privacy and national security concerns. In addition, the High Court ruled that information about the NSPA's organization, whereabouts and personnel were secrets that deserved to be kept confidential. The budget of the NSPA, the High Court ruled, should not be disclosed, in accordance with the NSPA Law. The National Assembly reviewed the budget in a closed session.[29]

On July 12, 2007, an NGO, the Lawyers for a Democratic Society, filed a suit against the minister of foreign affairs after the Ministry of Foreign Affairs declined the organization's request to disclose documents exchanged between the United States and South Korea during their negotiation over a Free Trade Agreement (FTA). The U.S.–South Korean negotiations for an FTA started in February 2006, when the two sides exchanged a draft agreement composed of 22 chapters. Two months later, the two sides agreed to classify all documents produced in the process of FTA negotiations for three years and allowed access to staff members who were in charge of relevant work, including ratification, on the condition of signing an affidavit pledging to maintain secrecy. After a series of negotiations, the two sides announced the conclusion of negotiations on April 2, 2007, and publicized an agreement on May 27, 2007. Faced with domestic criticism, South Korea pursued renegotiation, and on June 30, 2007, the two sides signed a revised agreement.

Lawyers for a Democratic Society requested information,

copies or emails regarding six newly inserted or changed chapters after comparing the original draft with the revised version. Instead of a direct response to the association within 20 days from the request date, the Foreign Ministry posted on its website its decision not to disclose requested information. In an internet posting titled "Notification of a decision regarding the request for disclosure of information," the ministry argued that the documents produced and exchanged in the process of negotiation could endanger important national interests if disclosed. Thus, in accordance with Article 9–1–2 of the Public Information Act, it concluded that the requested information belonged to the category of nondisclosed information.

The Seoul Administrative Court, on April 16, 2008, ruled the requested information belonged to "the category of information regarding foreign relations" stipulated by Article 9–1–2 of the Public Information Act, and further ruled that disclosure of information regarding specific arguments/counterarguments and negotiation positions exchanged between the United States and South Korea during the additional negotiation process would result in damage to grave national interests by providing valuable negotiation tips to other countries in their future negotiations with South Korea. The court also indicated a disclosure would cause a conflict of interest with the United States, stating that the decision not to disclose the information promoted national interests by maintaining international consent about not disclosing any document produced in the process of negotiation. The court concluded that the Foreign Ministry's decision not to disclose the information was a lawful measure.

In so doing, the court clearly indicated all information regarding negotiations did not have to be disclosed to promote objectivity and transparency in concluding a trade agreement with a foreign country. The court also indicated that problems resulting from the lack of transparency from a decision not to disclose relevant information would be resolved through a closed session controlled by the National Assembly, composed of representatives of the citizenry.[30]

About a year before Lawyers for a Democratic Society filed a suit against the Foreign Ministry, two members of the National Assembly requested the ministry to disclose the American draft of the FTA. When the ministry declined their request, they filed a suit by arguing the Foreign Ministry's refusal was not consistent with the Public Information Law. The plaintiffs argued that they had requested the information for facilitating their jobs as lawmakers.

The Seoul Administrative Court ruled that the decision to decline the plaintiffs' request was not inconsistent with the Public Information Law because disclosure of information regarding matters pursuant to foreign relations could endanger national security. The court also explained that the two plaintiffs, as members of the National Assembly, were granted access to the requested documents. Kang Ki-kap, as a member of the Committee for Agriculture and Forestry, was granted access to the document when he made a request to the Ministry of Agriculture and Forestry. In addition, the requested documents along with other relevant dossiers were provided to the Special Committee on FTAs of the National Assembly, and when the committee was not in session, the documents were made available in the reading room of the committee. The court concluded the plaintiffs' request was not made in accordance with the National Assembly Law, which entitled the members to request relevant documents. Rather, the request was made in accordance with the Public Information Law not by the members of the National Assembly but by normal citizens.[31]

On November 28, 1987, Korean Airlines flight KAL858, flying from Baghdad to Bangkok via Abu Dhabi, exploded with 20 crew and 95 passengers on board four hours and 20 minutes after taking off from Abu Dhabi Airport. The then National Security Planning Agency arrested two North Korean spies, Kim Hyon-hi and Kim Sung-il, who were disguised as a Japanese father and daughter. The agency sent the case to the Prosecutor's Office after concluding that, before leaving the plane at Abu Dhabi, the convicted had left a radio armed with liquid explosives which were set to explode during the flight between Abu Dhabi and Bangkok. The Supreme Court handed down a capital sentence to the accused on March 27, 1990. Kim Hyon-hi was discharged after she received a presidential special pardon in April 1990. Twelve years after the special pardon, bereaved family members raised doubts about the identity of Kim Hyon-hi and her confessed itinerary and requested the disclosure of all relevant information regarding the case. When the court declined the request, one of the bereaved family members, Cha Ok-jung, filed a suit against the chief prosecutor of the Seoul Central District Court.

The court ruled that some information could not be disclosed because it could threaten national interests regarding foreign relations and could also endanger the personal safety of arrested North Korean spies living in South Korea after their arrest. More specifically, it could hinder Japanese prosecutors in their investigation of North Korean spies operating in Japan. However, the court also ruled for the release of other information, such as the identities of Kim Hyon-hi and her accomplice, whose names were already widely known to public. In addition, the investigation records of foreign prosecution agencies as well as the domestic police could be released because they rarely endangered foreign relations or ongoing operations for investigating and arresting North Korean spies.[32]

## Legal Prosecution for Leakers

There are several institutional measures to prohibit unauthorized disclosures. The most immediate forms are contracts and statutes. When signing contracts and statutes, employees are asked to agree to respect statutes and other regulations that prohibit unauthorized disclosure or leakage of classified information. In addition, in some cases, intelligence officers are required to sign a nondisclosure agreement before gaining access to classified information. Signing the agreement automatically obliges signatories to refrain from unauthorized disclosure of classified information and at the same time serves as grounds for contractual dismissal and legal prosecution.[33] In the United States, those who commit unauthorized disclosures may face legal prosecution on the basis of two criminal statutes. First, disclosure of such sensitive secrets as communication intelligence, identities of covert agents and nuclear weapons data is strictly prohibited by specific statutes. Second, in more general terms, the Espionage Act and antitheft statutes prohibit disclosure of sensitive classified information.

The 2011 revision of South Korea's Military Secret Protection Law stipulates that an oath by a military officer to observe military secrecy remains valid even after his/her retirement, which implies that leaking information acquired before retirement is subject to legal prosecution. This revision was designed to block leaks from retired officers with security clearances who acquired sensitive classified information while serving.

On February 9, 2010, the local court of Changwon found retired and commissioned officers guilty as charged for leaking classified information acquired during their service on board the ROKS *King Sejong*.[34] The rule was designed to prohibit unauthorized leaks by retired officers who possessed security clearances during their service. These officers were charged with providing digital records of a Military Secret III in the form of a CD or USB saved without permission during their time in the military. They saved the content of classified information to the hard disks and in their personal folders. These officers were charged with saving information about the combat operational system of the ROKS *King Sejong* and related surface-to-air missiles without permission.

In 2006, the Supreme Court acknowledged that the inspection record issued by the Board of Audit and Inspection over the government project to import multipurpose helicopters could be regarded as a military secret, reversing the ruling by the Seoul Administrative Court, which had indicated only a procedural deficiency. In September 2005, the Seoul Administrative Court had ruled that the decision not to publicize the result of the inspection of the government project to import made-for-Korea multipurpose helicopters should be reversed. The presidential body assigned with oversight of the government's administrative behavior, upon receiving the request to publicize the report, refused to do so because the report contained secrets classified as Military Secret II and, accordingly, because disclosing the report would jeopardize national security. The Seoul Administrative Court indicated a procedural deficiency, in that the request should have been delivered to the Minister of Defense, who had authority over the release of the report. Then, the court ruled that, after the minister's evaluation of the impact on national security, the report was to be publicized. The local administrative court's ruling was reversed in November 2006 by the Supreme Court, which ruled that the request to publicize the board's report in accordance with the Public Information Act should not be acknowledged as a legal request on the basis of the Military Secret Protection Law.[35]

In January 2000, the Supreme Court pronounced the defendant guilty as charged for leaking military secrets. The accused was an officer at army headquarters who was in charge of army airpower projects including Ch-470D helicopters, MODE-4 surveillance radar, reconnaissance helicopters, UH-60 battalion equipment, and MISTAR land-to-air missiles. An arms dealer asked him to review a project involving optics equipment for helicopters, with the promise of financial reward. In return, the accused provided relevant information on GRC-17 radios for coast R/D bases, K-1 tanks and self-propelled artillery, which were all classified. The Supreme Court ruled that the accused was guilty of leaking military secrets and of bribery, even though the information he provided was not under his direct supervision.[36]

In the 1993 Mount Wangchaesan case, the Supreme Court ruled that information regarding U.S. forces' field manuals, simulation games, and operational plans to deal with an armed insurrection inside South Korea could not be acknowledged as factors threatening national security.[37] In South Korea, military secrets are

69

legally categorized into three levels. Level I secrets include military secrets designed to protect national security from potentially "critical" dangers. Level II secrets protect against "clear and present" dangers, while Level III secrets protect the nation from "considerable" dangers. Normally, Level I secrets contain sensitive information that could cause a war with other countries when leaked or disclosed. Secrets on other levels are said to endanger national security when leaked. However, court decisions do not always admit that information which may not appear secret in content could jeopardize national security.

In the Mount Wangchaesan case, the court found the defendant not guilty on the charge of organizing an antigovernment organization and instead found the defendant guilty as charged for individual espionage activity. Mount Wangchaesan is one of North Korea's revolutionary sites, where Kim Il Sung was known to have convened underground communist cadres in 1933 to enlarge the anti–Japanese struggle. Mr. Kim (full name not disclosed) was charged with allegedly forming an underground antigovernment organization in August 1993 under direct instruction from Kim Il Sung. The NSA consolidated evidence that Mr. Kim and four others pledged allegiance to Kim Il Sung, collected military information such as field manuals of U.S. forces as well as their simulation games, and set up a strategy for armed antigovernment insurrection inside South Korea. The court handed down a not-guilty verdict for lack of evidence on the charge of forming antigovernment organizations and also ruled that the information collected hardly threatened national security. However, the court sentenced the defendant guilty on the charge of espionage activity, which resulted in a seven-year prison term for Mr. Kim, in addition to seven years of suspended citizenship and four or five years in prison for other defendants.[38]

In August 2009, Mr. Kim, a retired marine who worked at a maritime product exchange company in Indonesia, was charged with providing compact disks containing a South Korean passport and detailed maps of South Korea, along with his ID and a password for an internet site for veterans. In accordance with the National Security Law, the charge against him also included behavior that encouraged and praised North Korea by the writing of a letter congratulating Kim Jong-il on his birthday. The local court sentenced Mr. Kim to two years in prison and three years' probation by ruling that Mr. Kim was not only guilty of providing information to North Korea but also of delivering a congratulatory letter to Kim Jong-Il. TheHigh Court maintained the same sentence—two years in prison along with three years' probation. However, it found the defendant not guilty on the charge of praising North Korea, in accordance with National Security Law.[39]

The High Court ruling was reversed by the Supreme Court, which ruled that Mr. Kim's behavior endangered national security and democratic order and returned the case to the High Court. The Supreme Court acknowledged that Mr. Kim's letter delivered a congratulatory message and maintained that Mr. Kim's behavior constituted a crime because it praised, encouraged and helped spread propaganda about the Kim Jong-il regime and expressed a desire to follow Kim Jong-il's overall policies, including his unification strategy.[40]

In 1997, on the charge of unauthorized entry into North Korea, the Supreme Court handed down guilty verdicts because the accused had met North Korean officials and praised their behavior and policies with the knowledge that such behavior could endanger national existence, national security and democratic order.[41]

## Respecting the Professionalism of Intelligence Officials

Legal judgment based on lawfulness and legitimacy can override classification decisions made by professional intelligence officials who acquired their skills through professional training and years of experience earned from governmental duties assigned

through constitutional procedures. Relying purely on legal judgment can conflict with constitutional separation of legal, administrative and parliamentary powers. This is why introduction of a
regulatory mechanism is recommended. At the same time, such
regulatory mechanisms always alarm intelligence officials about
problems that may be caused through unauthorized leaks or over-
classification.[42]

Still, there is another opinion. Judge Raymond Fisher in the
U.S. maintained the position that deferring to secret privileges was
to abandon independence of the courts based on the constitutional
principle of checks and balances, which would put civil liberties in
jeopardy. Procedural innovations through modification of trial procedures such as inviting outside experts or establishing special
courts staffed by judges and clerks specializing in foreign and security issues could be an option that would free the courts from the
burden of security clearances. As Robert Chesney observed, both
government officials and court judges tend to oversimplify the conflict between secret privileges and judicial review. He suggested
closer examination over the reasons why judges defer to executive
claims of secret privileges.[43]

The concern here is not about whether judges and their clerks
may be trusted or not. Rather, as Sagur indicates, the question is
whether the courts are equipped with appropriate capabilities to
deal with highly sensitive information; otherwise, the judicial review
process may lead to unauthorized or inadvertent leaks. In addition,
a court that routinely handles classified information will become
an easy target for espionage operations by foreign intelligence agencies. It requires professional knowledge with a sufficient period of
experience in security affairs to estimate or measure the harm generated by the disclosure of classified documents, which is different
from political judgments based on political awareness, morality and
common sense.[44]

It is also apparent that judges lack sufficient professional knowledge to tell whether the disclosure of certain secret information

would harm national security or how much harm such a disclosure would produce. Courts are generalist institutions composed of generalist judges. Few judges have significant experience in the field before being appointed to the federal or national bench. In fact, circulation of posts prevents further specialization or accumulation of experience. Judges are not trained to make judgments about costs and benefits of a disclosure to national security. Rather, they are there to produce norms and regulations about how to exercise privileges related to secrecy. Rather than stating when and how secrets should be disclosed or barred from disclosure, they need to provide rational reasons in defense of either secrecy or disclosure. Doing so would allow them to "moderate the scope and scale of state secrecy." Justice Robert Jackson observed at the *Chicago & Southern Air Lines v. Waterman SS Corp* (1948) case that such decisions should be made by professional intelligence officials who are "directly responsible to the people whose welfare they advance or imperil."[45]

The Supreme Court in *United States v. United States District Court* (1972), also known as "the Keith case," demonstrated that the concern was about "limited institutional capacity" which was "ill-equipped to handle large volumes of classified materials on an ongoing basis." While ruling to disclose unlawful wiretaps, the Supreme Court made it clear that the decision applied only to domestic issues and that foreign intelligence operations were not bound by the same standards. *Ellsberg v. Mitchell* (1983) also identified the problem not as the incapacity or lack of credibility of judges, lawyers or their clerks but as the lack of a sufficient level of equipment to deal with highly sensitive information. Even in a high-profile racial discrimination case brought by an employee of the CIA, *Sterling v. Tenet* (2005), identification of the person who was accused of discrimination for disclosing personal files of the CIA—a very basic necessary step for the investigation—was impossible because the court cited Reynolds's rule against *in camera* review of highly sensitive secret information. Jeffrey Sterling's equal employment lawsuit accusing his superior of racial discrimination was dismissed because there was no way to prove employment discrimination without exposing classified details of covert employment. The Fourth Circuit warned that the court was not supposed to "play with fire" when "advertent, mistaken or even intentional" disclosure would harm the very purpose of why the secret privilege existed. Sterling was indicted in 2010 for revealing national defense information to an unauthorized person, author and journalist James Risen, and was arrested in 2011. The FBI had intercepted email communication between Sterling and Risen during the period from 2002 to 2004. He was sentenced in 2015 to three and a half years in prison. *El-Masri v. United States* (2007) also indicated the comparative advantage of specialized intelligence agencies in evaluating the scale of harm a disclosure would cause. Khalid El-Masri held dual citizenship in Germany and Lebanon and was mistakenly arrested by Macedonian police and handed over to the CIA. He was then brought to a black site in Afghanistan, where he was "interrogated, beaten, strip-searched, sodomized" and subjected to other inhumane treatment. After the CIA concluded his arrest and torture were a mistake, he was released and proceeded to file suit. However, rather than questioning the intellectual competence of judges, the Fourth Circuit explained that executive officers in the field of foreign and security affairs were capable of making "more refined and accurate predictive judgments" about the disclosure of sensitive secret information and its impact on national security.[46]

To overcome these shortcomings, several measures have been recommended. First, appointment of experienced staff with appropriate security clearances to legal positions in the courts could facilitate the process of dealing with classified information and of evaluating secret privilege based on mosaic theory. Second, Fuchs and Posen also suggest a classified judicial forum inside Congress in which judges and legal officials ad litem hear state secret cases *in camera* on a permanently sealed and bench-trial basis. Legal officials may be selected from a group of federal public defenders with appropriate security clearances. Fuchs emphasizes the autonomy of outside experts, in that they should be independent of any current or future relationship with either intelligence agencies or plaintiffs because their main task would be to winnow down large volumes of records, a basic but critical stage before trials.[47]

However, the introduction of a judicial forum as a parliamentary body by inviting outside experts would not be without its flaws. It is obvious that possession of security clearances with professional knowledge implies that the candidates would have been former government intelligence agents. For them, maintenance of security clearances remains an attractive incentive to cooperate with government agencies because losing the clearance implies disconnection from a daily supply of classified information. Selection of someone with little connection with the government means a lack of updated knowledge on current security concerns. Again, dependence on judges with little professional knowledge of security issues would be the most viable choice.[48]

In addition, deep secrets generate more complications. *Phillippi v. CIA* (1975)[49] dealt with "deep secrets" by showing that intelligence officials were entitled to claim that acknowledging the mere existence of a secret could harm national security. Moreover, it also showed that explanations of why acknowledging their existence could harm national security itself could harm national security. In this case, journalist Harriet Phillippi, by requesting relevant information from the CIA, tried to confirm the existence of a covert operation reportedly conducted by a ship, the *Glomar Explorer,* in search of a sunken Soviet submarine. The CIA responded negatively by stating that the existence of such activity that was in the interest of national security could not be confirmed or denied, which triggered Phillippi's approach to the district court. For Phillippi, getting the CIA to provide a detailed justification of why documents on the operation should be withheld would suffice for her purpose of confirming the existence of the operation. The CIA submitted classified affidavits that led the court to issue a summary judgment in favor of the CIA. Then, Phillippi approached the D.C. Circuit requesting an examination of those documents on the details of classified operation, not just the affidavits. The D.C. Circuit also rejected her claim by concluding that courts were entitled to examine only classified affidavits *in camera* without plaintiff's counsel when the government held an NCND position about the existence of the requested documents.

In South Korea, courts tend not to acknowledge the professionalism of the intelligence community and the validity of the mosaic theory. The Constitutional Court mentioned that the realm of classification of information should be restricted to the smallest extent necessary so that the freedom of expression and the right to know could be guaranteed to the maximum possible degree. The Constitutional Court further mentioned that classification does not mean classified content should be regarded as military secrets because Articles 2 and 3 hardly seem to bestow almighty or exclusive authority to classify all military affairs. It does not mean classification of military information in accordance with the Military Secret Protection Law is legally ineffective; however, the realm of military secrecy should be legally interpreted as narrowly as possible to protect the citizenry's right to know.

In 1992, the Constitutional Court of Korea in its ruling raised the necessity of comparing what can be gained by respecting secrecy with losses arising from limiting the people's right to know. In a case involving one of the staff working for a National Assembly member, the Constitutional Court ruled that Articles 6, 7, and 10 of the Military Secret Protection Law were not unconstitutional. In doing so, the Constitutional Court admitted leaking documents marked as "Military Secret" on their cover pages could endanger national security. In this case, a staff member of a National Assembly member was charged for leaking military secrets which he acquired illegally. The staff appealed to the Constitutional Court that the Military Secret Protection Law was unconstitutional for imposing limits on a citizen's right to know.

While ruling for the Military Secret Protection Law, the Constitutional Court signaled the need to construct a nationwide consensus by sharing military information with the public. The Constitutional Court also mentioned there are cases in which classified information poses little danger to national security. Even in cases when there are reasonable grounds to classify certain information, the Constitutional Court elaborated, one has to consider if what is gained from classifying information does not overshadow the damage caused by limiting the people's right to know. Rather, according to the rule, inviting positive participation from the public on major security decisions could contribute to national security by constructing citizen consensus on important national security policies.

# 4

# The Media and National Security

What marked the turning point in the relationship between the media and national security in South Korea, as mentioned in the introductory chapter, were the junctures between post–Cold War culture and continued confrontation with North Korea on the one hand and between globalization and democratization on the other. The perceptional taboo that had prohibited open discussion on national security was lifted. At the same time, a gradual decrease of government control over information flow regarding national security and an increase of media influence were accompanied by the spread of the internet and social media.

Still, compared with other countries, security-media links in South Korea present a unique picture: Strict government monopoly of military information and a higher degree of public tolerance towards government control. While 9/11 revived the Cold War paradigm in the United States, the Cold War never ended in South Korea, and its paradigm serves as the guideline of media reporting on foreign and security issues. Much in the way the United States government needs media cooperation to reduce elite dissent and negative public opinion in the war against terror, the South Korean government also requires its media to observe certain criteria when reporting stories on security and foreign affairs, especially on North Korean and military affairs.[1]

Right after democratization, the South Korean media still

maintained a strong tendency to adopt pro-government frames in covering foreign and security issues. The South Korean media in the 1990s demonstrated the overwhelming influence of newspapers compared with TV news networks. Censorship over TV news content by the military authoritarian regime in the 1980s meant that the first stories of everyday TV news were about the presidents, Chun Doo Hwan and Roh Tae Woo, which decreased the credibility of TV news a great deal.

In discussing the influence of the media on foreign and security affairs, whether or not a policy change takes place due to media coverage has drawn much scholarly attention. Quite often, a successful foreign policy requires, to a certain degree, cooperation by the media. It is especially so when the president is sensitive to media coverage of his policy. For example, the former president Kim Young Sam, during his term, exerted influence on newspapers by reading most newspaper stories. Before being elected in 1992, he had for more than 30 years been a democratic leader who was often labeled as having an inborn instinct to read the public's mind. Even after he was elected, he was still sensitive to his approval ratings and the flow of public opinion. One of the top priorities in the pursuit of policy alternatives during his term was to acquire public endorsement through favorable coverage by the media.

It has long been a widely accepted idea that decision makers are influenced by what they regard as important at the moment of decision making. In addition, they are conditioned by their educational backgrounds, perceptions, and values that have been formulated through their experiences. Preexisting values, prejudices and emotions toward a specific country especially affect their policy-making.[2] A typical politician who is anxious about their public image is affected by the concern of how their policies are reported by the media. Douglas Hurd, former British secretary of state for foreign affairs, after a foreign policy statement to the House of Commons, usually retired to the studios across the road for "five or six interviews on the trot, four for television and two for radio." He confessed that the procedure became "almost part of the constitution." Such an "arduous and sometimes tiresome routine" is endured not entirely due to the anxiety to inform the public, nor due to concerns over one's image, but in part due to the realization that if one does not give an interview when invited, the time for the interview could be replaced by critical comments over one's policy. Indeed, the way events and opinions are reported affects policymakers through two concentric circles. On the inside of the circle, policymakers take actions reported by the media, which in turn are read and reabsorbed by the policymakers, who may or may not modify their policy. On the outside of the circle, reports on events and policies draw public reaction, and responses are fed back to the policymakers via their elected representatives. Although the policy-makers have the initiative, they are in large part conditioned by media reporting. Regardless of whether they change their policies or not in the face of media criticism or even public response, the policymakers are nonetheless greatly conditioned by the media.[3]

It is also notable that media audiences tend to interpret media texts not in terms of long-term national interests, nor in accordance with policy rationale, but in light of stereotypical interpretations set by the media. For a governmental official, communicating the rationale of public policy is an essential prerequisite to public office; a foreign policy official cannot be an exception. However, the rationale of a policy is often painted by the SOPs and profit-making mechanisms of the media. The result leads to a somewhat different conclusion. What is important is how the pictures will look, whether the public will be impressed by the swiftness of the leader's response and whether it will cause favorable public response—not whether the policy promotes long-term national interests.

Here, the term "democracy without citizens" is worth discussing. With a president who is sensitive to how their government is covered by the media, government officials have no choice but to heed attention to how their policy is covered by the media.

Some 70.8 percent of the reporters at the Foreign Ministry press-room in 1997 indicated that they had a certain, although not deci-sive, degree of influence over the speed and direction of policymaking and implementation. To a more explicit question, "do you have an experience of killing a policy before it is publicized or supporting a policy by playing a decisive role in getting public endorsement?" 45.8 percent of the reporters confirmed that they had such experi-ence.[4]

Although South Korea is a divided country where foreign and security affairs can influence the daily lives of citizens, domestic politics usually draw more media attention. Even in the midst of North Korea's nuclear quagmire, what has drawn more attention than the nuclear threat was Kim Young Sam's personal capability to deal with North Korea and his overall leadership to manage state affairs.

This is why coverage of foreign and security affairs is usually "dramatic and sensational" on the one hand and "trivial and super-ficial" on the other.[5] In order to introduce major foreign policy issues, most stories have to be "too brief, too fast-paced, and too devoid of perspectives in order to facilitate comprehension by the public."[6] The politics department of each newspaper, for its part, has to boil down hard and complicated news like foreign affairs into box coverage on inner pages while putting stories on domestic pol-itics like behind-the-scenes negotiations and power struggles on the front page. Some 45.8 percent of the reporters at the Foreign Ministry have complained that articles on foreign affairs occupy an insufficient ratio, while 8.3 percent rated the coverage extremely insufficient. Another 45.8 percent indicated that the ratio of foreign affairs stories in the press reports is about appropriate.

Beyond the president, various groups try to insert their influ-ence on the policy agenda. The media plays the role of vehicle for many groups, including the National Assembly. For many interest groups, particularly the resource-poor, media attention may be the only vehicle to gain recognition as legitimate policy actors. Their ultimate objective is to set or change the policy agenda in their favor through communicating their messages to the public, which requires media coverage. The scope and influence of interest groups are by and large limited because their strength comes only from their ability to publicize their issues widely through the media. If the interest groups are successful, the media transmit news to foreign media.

Members of the National Assembly are generally more open to the media than are government officials. In the National Assembly, even the most junior staffer regularly contacts reporters. In addition, there are often several competing groups in the legislature, one of which may be willing to form an alliance with reporters. Those younger members from both the National Assembly and the media are likely to find they are of the same generation and have a common frame of reference. Therefore, younger politicians usually seek out the media for favorable media coverage in return for hot news items. In addition, for any legislative member, a successful election campaign requires good and timely media support. Lastly, the National Assembly and the media provide each other with the legitimacy to challenge the bureaucracy. Congressional inquiry into a certain affair in which members of the bureaucracy are involved allows a reporter to continue the chase. Similarly, members of the National Assembly, even powerful leaders, are usually reluctant to challenge the president unless they are empowered by media reports. As Simon Serfaty points out, "legislators and journalists share a common rivalry against the executives as they all seek to discover what the executive is up to, uncover wrongdoing, or expose inherent contradictions in policies or their implementation." All these factors contribute to form a symbiotic relationship between the National Assembly and the media. Other observations indicate that even without elections to be won or legislation to be passed, members of the legislature have good reason to rush to the media. Media coverage provides congressional members with celebrity, an image most politicians want to have. The "I am on TV therefore I

am" syndrome common to most politicians is in some part the crea-
ture of the media.[7]

# Pulling and Hauling in the Past Symbiosis Between the Media and the Government

In the 1990s and early 2000s, most press releases from the government were scheduled before noon to provide newspaper
reporters with ample time to write stories by 5:00 p.m., the deadline
for submitting articles for street editions. Scheduling important
announcements in the afternoon gave limited time to write stories
and would result in less friendly and highly critical contents. Then,
around 7:30 in the evening, young government officials from each
ministry began gathering in the streets of Gwanghwamun, where
they could purchase street editions of the next morning's newspapers. The young officials purchased a set of all street-edition newspapers and hurried back to their offices. After roughly an hour,
telephones started ringing with phone calls from government sectors requesting corrections, rewritings or removal of stories before
the president would read those stories. Newspapers' refusal to
rewrite or remove stories could lead to reproach from the presidential office.

Competition and cooperation between the media and the
government became conspicuous after the first edition of the
next morning's issue was delivered in the evening around 7:30 or
8:00. One of the main functions of night desks was to receive phone
calls from governments requesting deletion of or changes to articles
and often titles. Most requests for changing the content of or even
deleting articles were generally accepted, but changing titles was
another story. In newspapers, the politics section was usually in
charge of foreign affairs and was responsible for the coverage of
foreign policy issues, but it was the editorial section that composed
the title of every article. Changing titles and stories should be

decided through night chiefs, who functioned on behalf of the editor-in-chief.

In the case of TV, in the absence of the first-edition paper, government officials requested cooperation for major foreign policy issues over the phone before stories were aired. Sometimes senior officials' requests included a desirable order of stories and timing for a specific story. Also, most requests tended to be accepted. Checking the contents of the 9:00 news before it was aired was very difficult unless the government monitored Q-sheets beforehand. However, not only because the broadcasting companies did not send Q-sheets to the government but because Q-sheets themselves were subject to change five minutes before 9:00, the mechanism that worked for newspapers did not work for TV news.

In addition, the extremely high competition among ten newspaper publishing companies all targeting the Seoul metropolitan area makes South Korea a heaven of "herd journalism." This phenomenon refers to the tendency of the press to cover the same events in much the same way, ignoring other developments and issues. Under the circumstances set by herd journalism, the worst thing a reporter can do is to have a "dropped" story, as opposed to an "exclusive" story. All newspaper editors have to check what rival newspapers report by reading their street edition newspapers. If there is any "dropped story," they deliberately write their own version of the same story after reading their rival's original story. Every newspaper knows that an exclusive story on the first edition is likely to be copied. If a big story is placed in a street edition, this gives other newspapers more time to read the content, send their reporters and write their own version of the story in their very next edition.

The media and the government formed a symbiosis, a relationship that was mutually beneficial and exploitive.[8] It was Cohen who conceptualized the term "symbiosis" in his book in 1963. It later evolved into the term "co-evolution" of interdependent mutual exploitation by O'Heffernan.[9] Interdependence evolves between reporters who always need hot and juicy information and government officials who in turn need favorable coverage. Mutually exploitive reporters and officials enter into a game of pulling and hauling in which they carefully calculate costs and benefits. Whether to provide information in the form of leaks or whether to report leaked information that could harm government positions depends on the result of the calculation. On the government side, what is prioritized are national interests, secrecy, bureaucratic interests or personal interests of the official in charge, while on the media side, exclusive stories, newsworthiness and profit-making mechanisms of media companies are prioritized. When reporters break "off-the-record" or "embargoed" information, cost-benefit calculation involves the risks of alienating important information sources versus publishing an exclusive cover story.

In South Korea, there are various parochial factors that facilitate cooperation between reporters and government officials. Like the coalition formed between legislative members and reporters, government officials may have similar relations with reporters through common educational background (*Hak-yon*) and hometown (*chi-yon*), which results from the unique culture of Korean parochialism. In addition, as the number of politicians who were previously journalists indicates, the bigger the chances for journalists to enter into politics by endorsement from the ruling party, the more cooperation the government gets from them. Lastly, considering the special implications of security in Korea, not a small portion of information with regard to foreign affairs is off-limits for reporting due to national security planning. In order to scoop off-limits information, the media has no choice but to acquiesce to government requests for either changing or deleting articles.

Negative media coverage exerts significant pressure, especially in cases where it gains widespread attention from the public.[10] In some cases, television pictures and large newspaper articles are sensationally dramatized and accompany political pressures to "do something."[11]

Through this practice, the media reports constrain government policy options and set the pace of policy development. Media reports on conflict between foreign policymakers tend to cause a negative impact on public attitude toward the government.[12] Indeed, at the early stage of the Kim Young Sam government, one subject the press liked to report was conflict between top policymakers.

## *Media Frames on Foreign and Security Issues*

It is almost impossible to find an "unframed" story. Doris Graber defined the media frame as "reporting the news from a particular perspective so that some aspects of the situation come into close focus and others fade into the background,"[13] while Shanto Iyengar defined it as "subtle alterations in the statement or presentation of judgment and choice problems."[14] By framing stories, the media define boundaries of debates by placing a certain case "within a certain sphere of meaning."[15] In doing so, the media influence the screening process of media users in which they perceive, understand and remember a certain incident, thereby affecting and guiding their judgment and responses.[16] It is the media-generated version of a debate that draws attention from the public and confers legitimacy upon a particular aspect of reality while "marginalizing" other aspects.[17]

Robert Entman introduced the most conspicuous comparison of frames by illuminating the difference in American media's frames over two similar incidents: the Soviet shooting down of Korean Air Lines flight 007, killing 269 passengers and crew on September 1, 1983, and USS *Vincennes'* shooting down of Iran Air 655, killing 290 passengers and crew on July 3, 1988. The American media portrayed the former incident as "Murder in the Air," "A Ruthless Ambush in the Sky," "Shooting to Kill," and "Atrocity in the Skies" while constructing a totally different frame for the latter incident by focusing on "Why It Happened" and "What Went Wrong in the Gulf."[18]

The South Korean media has demonstrated similar trends. For example, report coverage of a sexual abuse case by a North Korean Olympic official participating in the 1996 Atlanta Olympics showed stark differences before and after the so-called submarine incident. When the North Korean official was charged for physically touching an American child, the South Korean media represented warm inter–Korean relations by employing a frame that molded a sympathetic atmosphere. The media highlighted the differences between American and Korean cultures.[19] The Olympics took place roughly four months after Presidents Bill Clinton and Kim Young Sam had proposed the four-party talks in April 16, 1996, at Jeju Island. While the two countries expected North Korea's participation in the four-party talks, North Korea's participation in the Olympics could have led to improved inter–Korean and U.S.–North Korean relations.

Two months later when the North Korean official departed the United States in secret, the South Korean media constructed a frame criticizing the illegal departure and the sexually abusive behavior of the official.[20] The change in frames was due to the inter–Korean tension heightened by a stranded North Korean infiltration submarine on the eastern coast in September. The South Korean military launched a massive operation searching for North Korean commandos. Sixteen South Korean soldiers were killed and inter–Korean relations became stalemated until North Korea apologized by expressing regrets.

The South Korean media has a strong tendency to portray dichotomous frames of two contrasting concepts: good and bad, conservative and liberal, young and old, rich and poor, ruling and opposition, pro–North Korean and anti–North Korean, protestors and police, or us and them. Which side of the two extremes triggers public support is situational and dependent on media frames with approval-enhancing or approval-diminishing effects.[21] In some cases, the media depict protestors as deviant outlaws and in others as citizen demonstrators protesting against excessive abuse of authority.

Scholarly debate illustrates two contrasting views on the influence of the media on public opinion. One demonstrates media's intentional influence on government decisions by driving public opinion in a specific direction, and the other illustrates government's deliberate control of the media by providing selective information. As a questionnaire of the South Korean reporters demonstrates, the media does exercise influence on the government. More than a few cases have witnessed the media's independent influence on foreign and security policy. Although media coverage is not a direct representation of public opinion, the first impression of an incident reported by the media frames public perception, thereby playing a pivotal role as "the conduit, the pipeline, the funnel" of the flow of secret information.[22]

On the other hand, the media usually frames reports on foreign and security affairs in ways that reflect national interests and promote public support. A typical contrast in frames is the deficiency of an aircraft versus mistakes of pilots when there is a landing incident or aircraft crash. Quite often, the media stimulate national sentiment such as anti–Americanism in reporting U.S. military personnel crimes against female Korean victims or anti–Japan sentiment by raising issues like the Dok-do (Takeshima in Japanese) and Yasukuni Shrines. In particular, the accident in which two 13-year-old girls were killed by a 50-ton Bradley armored vehicle triggered anti–American sentiment in the Korean media, which will be discussed in detail later. The contrast in TV and newspaper coverage on the issue will also be discussed later. Similar coverage appears in the Japanese and American media. The Japanese media also demonstrate an anti–American stance when they cover such issues as U.S. bases in Okinawa and U.S. military personnel sexual crimes. For their part, the American media appeared to show biased frames in covering the war in Iraq by focusing on how fast American troops advanced toward Baghdad, rather than on civilian losses and destruction.

Media coverage may be split into three categories. News content may represent one side's dominating views. Or coverage may arbitrate and amalgamate various views. Lastly, some coverage generates its own version of debate. In generating its own version of reality, the media plays the dual roles of civic conduit between the government and the public and that of an independent engine by inputting its own interpretation.[23] By playing the role of government megaphone, the media justifies government policy toward North Korea and at the same time marginalizes other views and opinions.[24] When exercising an independent journalistic influence, South Korean media affects public opinion on North Korea and guides public judgment and responses by providing views different from government views.[25]

In South Korea, the media sometimes employs episodic frames to affect short-term dispositions. News frames determine mainstream views between anger against North Korean provocations and sympathy for starved children.[26] Through deliberate leaks of monopolized information, the government may manipulate media coverage. Leaks are still a more valuable information source than official announcements, which are easily sensationalized and personalized. Deliberate leaks serve as effective governmental tools for promoting and facilitating policy processes. Before a summit, leaks about a new proposal also attract reporters.[27]

Since information regarding security and North Korea is highly monopolized by the government, deliberate leaks are effective governmental tools to shape and angle media coverage, as McCloskey's Law indicates. In addition, by controlling the timing and range of leaks, the government may test public response and promote a policy under implementation.[28] Few reporters refuse to access leaked information as long as the information is exclusive.[29] A deliberate leak could also facilitate policy implementation and in some cases support the government's position during a negotiation with a foreign government. In 1996, negative public opinion toward North Korea supported South Korea's suspension of payment for light-water reactors to satisfy the KEDO (Korean Peninsula Energy Development Organization) agreement.

Geyelin posits that governments inherently hold the high ground in their relations with the media except in rare cases of scandal or malpractice of governmental authority. According to him, the media serves "as nothing more than a monitor or a megaphone" which transmits "propositions that a government wants to place on the agenda and of the debate such propositions may generate."[30] This is especially true when covering foreign and security policy because, except in certain cases, most issues do not draw wide public attention.

## North Korean Nuclear Issues

The media frame during the 1994 North Korean nuclear crisis demonstrated continued support for the government policy of calling for transparency. Newspapers stories expressed concern over excessive compensation by the United States only to facilitate the negotiation process and temporarily halt North Korea's nuclear development at the expense of South Korea's long-term national security. Until the signing of the Agreed Framework that halted North Korea's nuclear activity without concern for "breakout time," the main theme of newspaper stories focused on the possibility of North Korea's possession of nuclear bombs.

Right after the signing of the Agreed Framework, many articles focused on the lack of reliable measures to guarantee the transparency of North Korea's nuclear activity and concerns over breakout time. Newspapers stories covered criticisms by the members of the National Assembly during their annual audit inspection.

Then, herd journalism switched the main theme from the nuclear program to economic investment in the North. This was also in support of the government's position, as the Kim Young Sam government launched a massive investment program in North Korea in an attempt to avoid media criticism for having done nothing for more than a year while the United States and North Korea negotiated in Geneva. The death of Kim Il-Sung triggered Bill Clinton's expression of regrets and condolences to the Korean people for their loss of their leader, which was regarded by North Korea as the official condolences.

## OECD Membership

Another example that shows media frames in support of the government may be found in stories covering South Korea's application for OECD membership. Its application for observer membership in three committees of the OECD in February 1993 was accepted by unanimous OECD board decision in October 1996.[31] Then, the Kim Young Sam government wanted to raise its approval rate by portraying the membership as having the status equivalent of developed countries. In contrast, opposition parties led by Kim Dae-jung and Kim Jong-pil along with citizen organizations led by the Korean Citizen's Coalition for Economic Justice opposed the membership. They argued that the membership obliged the compulsory opening of domestic markets, which would be detrimental to the domestic economy.

The media appeared to maintain a balanced position between the pros and cons. Media criticisms against the membership were not strong enough to exert negative influence on the government policy. Opposition voices were also covered by the media under the title of "Opening a champagne bottle too early."

In fact, the media abstained from registering excessive criticism against the OECD membership except when the peso devaluation increased public concern over the negative effects of membership. Mostly, the media carried positive stories in covering the OECD review process that qualified South Korea in July 1996 and the unanimous vote that admitted South Korea. In sum, this was an exemplary case in which the media played the sincere role of megaphone of the government. It could successfully convince the citizens to perceive the membership as equivalent to a membership in the society of rich countries. Media criticisms through various articles, editorials, columns and op-ed pieces and dissent from opposition parties were deliberately balanced with supportive articles. As a result, the South Korean government enjoyed cooperation from the media.

## SOFA

One of the noticeable developments after democratization in the 1990s was the lifting of taboos in discussing security-related affairs. One of them was about the role of the U.S. forces in South Korea. As noted, domestic democratization and the end of the Cold War lowered public perception regarding the need of U.S.–South Korean alliance, while the perception of inequality over the Status of Forces Agreement (SOFA) increased. American military personnel crimes against Korean civilians, especially female victims, triggered public anger and demonstrations calling for the rewriting of SOFA.

Between August 1995, when South Korea suggested an amended version of SOFA, and December 1996, when bilateral negotiations to rewrite the agreement failed to reach any agreement, the South Korean media demonstrated a strong trend to represent national sentiment and anti–Americanism, which supported South Korea's negotiation position. The number of articles increased in October 1995, when the Washington visit of ROK foreign minister Gong Ro-Myong failed to elicit any agreement, in July 1996, when front pages were filled with stories about U.S. unilateral cancellation of the negotiations, and in September 1996, when the seventh round of SOFA negotiations ended without any agreement.

Media attention decreased dramatically in the fall of 1996 due to the infiltration of North Korean commandos after their spy submarine washed ashore. In this case, the media played dual roles. The media strengthened South Korea's negotiation position by carrying stories covering public discontent over the unequal aspects of the treaty. At the same time, the media criticized the lukewarm stance of the government by playing up the inferiority and lack of diplomatic capability of the government vis-à-vis the United States. For its part, the government registered concern over possible spillover influence on the U.S. forces stationed in South Korea and overall bilateral relations with Washington.[32]

## Food Aid to North Korea

The food aid to North Korea in 1995 drew massive media attention. On the day of shipping, the aid was described as the South's victory to help starved North Koreans on the day of the Korean War anniversary. Later, the aid was ridiculed as "being slapped for doing good," a sarcastic metaphor criticizing the Kim Young Sam government's North Korea policy. The media coverage of the food aid reached its peak when the first shipment to the North was made on June 25. Then, media coverage marked a dramatic downturn in August when news was released that the North Korean port authority had forced the first South Korean vessel to hoist the North Korean flag and had even seized the second ship because one of the crew had taken a photograph of the port.

In September and October, newspaper reports launched massive criticisms toward the Kim Young Sam government's North Korea policy, which led to the decision to halt any further food aid. The halt marked the turning point of Kim Young Sam's dovish policy toward North Korea, which led to a six-month-long deadlock in inter–Korean relations.

In South Korea, ideological and socioeconomic values on the

one hand and national sentiments on the other determine news frames.[33] In representing those values, the media's role is far from being a megaphone. Rather, the media represent the dominant climate of public opinion.[34] These values and sentiments define the directions of media frames, which in turn further infuriate the public. The press is not always satisfied with playing the role of megaphone. The role quickly changes "from that of megaphone to that of monitor—questioning, analyzing, and providing wider and more sophisticated perspectives from critics as well as supporters."[35]

## Dokdo and Anti-Japan Sentiment

The question of territorial sovereignty over Dokdo always draws media attention, along with issues of the comfort women and Yasukuni Shrine. In the general election in 1996, Japan's LDP (Liberal Democratic Party) selected the claim over the islands of Senkaku and Dokdo (Takeshima in Japanese) as its official election slogan, which triggered massive opposition in South Korea. The South Korean government wanted to silence the issue as much as possible to avoid internationalization of the issue, which could have turned the island into an area of international dispute. Bringing the issue to the International Court of Justice was the last thing South Korea wanted, and the Foreign Ministry concluded that further debate of the issue could be detrimental.

Contrary to governmental positions, the media wrote stories that kept on stimulating anti–Japan sentiment, as Japan-related issues usually reminded the Korean public of past memories of colonial rule and stimulated national sentiment against Japan. The media's massive campaign of criticisms against Japan prompted the South Korean government's official reaction. On September 30, Mr. Dae-won Suh, spokesman for the MOFA (Ministry of Foreign Affairs), issued an official statement criticizing the LDP.

He said the LDP's campaign slogan was irresponsible and would never be acceptable. On the following day, the Korean ambassador in Tokyo, Tae-chi Kim, visited the LDP and the Japanese Foreign Ministry to express official opposition against its campaign slogans.

# 5

# Social Media and National Security

The influence of the media on security and foreign affairs has followed a fundamentally new pattern in the era of social media. Symbiosis between reporters and government officials is now no longer valid. In the past, government officials and reporters maintained symbiotic relationships through the exchange of juicy bits of information and favorable coverage. Sometimes officials requested self-restraint in reporting in return for promising to serve as future sources of information.

Now, citizens capable of registering their own independent ideas weaken the symbiosis between reporters and officials. Interdependence between the media and the government over security issues is transformed in the process of dual transition between the Cold War paradigm and a new paradigm of the global War on Terror on the one hand and between conventional media and social media on the other. The transition also accompanies ideational confusion of the enemy/friend classification.

Social media is gradually replacing the role of the opinion leaders and elites who used to lead public opinion. For example, George W. Bush's vilification of North Korea by labeling it part of the "axis of evil" in 2002 complicated rather than dominated the world's perception of friends and enemies. While North Korea was labeled as evil, inter–Korean relations reached their peak, and social media users in South Korea generated positive views on North Korea.

How to define the media's legitimate role in public opinion usually accompanies similar questions of how to judge media performance and whether we like to see sensationalism in reporting about national security and North Korea. What security officials want is not visual information that either horrifies the public or makes it sympathetic. Rather, they want detailed contextual information so that public horror or sympathy does not lead to policy disapproval. The reality, though, shows an outflow of episodic frames wrapped with horrific or sympathetic images on the internet and social media. Thematic coverage that could educate uninformed citizens attracts few viewers and readers.[1]

Rhetorical statements on social media are more influential over public opinion, regardless of objective indicators of reality. Such influence, however, recedes fast when another version of rhetoric emerges on social media. As a result, the role of traditional media outlets as a common civic space is eroding.[2] What people want from social media is a counter-frame against authoritative government frames. The counter-frame is usually constructed of "culturally resonant words and images" widely shared within a society. Social media from time to time stimulate the watchdog instincts of traditional media reporters by introducing openly voiced dissent, which in turn forms a counter-frame against the government's skilled release of information. Counter-frames offer what would be a sensible alternative to government prescriptions to given situations. Those who trust social media believe that policymakers frame security to their own advantage and that the news to which they are exposed by traditional media outlets does not represent the true nature of what has happened. They believe social media takes what has been distorted and re-distorts it back to the "right" direction. In this process, media users "rarely" observe what really happens. Instead, what they see is a multi-framed representation of security events confused by the incentives of policymakers, professional journalistic standards of gatekeeping and social media reproduction of counter-frames.[3]

Social media often deals with security and foreign affairs in a way to involve top decision makers, the most authoritative and high-ranking sources, thereby satisfying one of the most important criteria for newsworthiness: public attention.[4] At the same time, involving top officials provides opportunities to criticize overall governmental incompetence to deal with individual dissatisfaction. This causes a competition between the government and social media over dominant frames. Political culture determines public reactions to certain events. Government frames usually control public opinion when issues at hand are culturally congruent or unambiguously incongruent. Social media coverage hardly exercises influence in molding public opinion when issues are obviously congruent or incongruent with prevailing political culture. However, when schemas with contradictory interpretations exist, political culture only provides ambiguous guidance. Under this circumstance, government frames lose control, while the influence of social media interpretation increases.[5]

When there is a strong majority opinion positively inclined to the government stance, antigovernment voices including those from social media tend to be non-influential, and intermittent coverage of opposing views hardly attracts public attention. Governmental monopoly of security information, control of timing and scope of disclosure make generating coherent counter-frame against government stances very difficult. "Red-baiting" is often used by some extreme conservatives to silence opposition activists and parliamentary members by distorting their ideological positions in ways to connect them with enemies.[6]

Diplomats can override framed media coverage and the consequent public anger because they have access to espionage data, behind-the-scenes negotiations and rational calculations of national interest. However, when the issue at hand is ambiguous or requires complicated explanation that hardly attracts public attention, oppositional comments of security policy by elites and celebrities satisfy social media interests. They offer great opportunities to set up counter-frames against government policies. Even when the oppositional comments fail to effectively challenge government policies, social media may spur a series of dissenting views, thereby igniting a competition for the dominant frame.[7]

Once a dominant frame is accepted by the public, a counter-frame promoted by government with official and confirmed evidence provides little guidance to an inexpert audience in developing their own independent interpretation. Government release of certain information is usually responded to by a counter-frame set by oppositional elites and celebrities through social media. No matter which frame dominates, traditional media outlets cover the initial stage of the frame competition. It usually takes a day or two before traditional media outlets bring new information to light based on facts. It is too late to generate a learning effect because the public has already been persuaded by either authoritative frames set by the government or counter-frames which have been adroitly and strategically infused by opposition figures.[8] When Barack Obama said that George W. Bush would "ignore facts" about Iraq, Obama emphasized the importance of "preconceived notions" embedded in American public opinion.[9]

It is more common in social media that distrust of the government is a dominant view and that most security issues are perceived to be fabricated by the government. Social media produces a different explanation of similar security affairs by approaching them in a totally different cultural context. Skepticism vis-à-vis government abuse of power and antigovernment repertoires is embedded in unconfirmed stories distributed through social media. On the other hand, the security-oriented conservative culture is buried in the news reported by traditional media outlets and cable news networks. Social media are more available for young and liberal users, while conservative cable news networks target the older generation.[10]

It is indicated that citizens depend on inaccurate representations of national security when they position themselves between national security and civil rights. Credibility of media messages is determined by their sources, the messengers conveying the message, the media outlets reporting the message, and the context within which the messages are delivered.[11] While young liberal citizens appear more receptive to messages delivered by social media and power bloggers, older conservative users prefer traditional outlets and cable news networks. Social media is a product generated by personal connections and social comparisons. Social media makes selective exposure and selective attention possible, which implies users see and listen only to what they want to see and listen to. In other words, they focus only on what attracts their attention.[12]

Citizens select ideologically friendly media outlets to which they are receptive while discounting reports delivered by ideologically hostile media. Citizens who are accustomed to only one side of a story become less and less willing to accept stories "at odds" with their preexisting values and beliefs. This results in a decrease of their willingness to reposition their ideological positions by compromising with varying ideas spread by ideologically hostile media.[13]

What is also notable is that characteristics found in soft news are embedded in social media coverage of security affairs. To put it simply, soft news is usually different from hard news delivered by conventional news outlets. Most citizens who are not interested in hard news and long stories are exposed to foreign and security issues while watching entertainment programs such as drama and comedy, which provide simple dichotomous definitions of right and wrong, good and bad or yes and no to complicated foreign policy questions.[14]

## Social Media and Security in South Korea

Social media in South Korea demonstrates a similar trend. First, young media users in South Korea are accustomed to getting news more from social media than from traditional media outlets. Second, different standards in story gatekeeping and editorial filtering usually provide more behind-the-scenes stories which would normally not be allowed to be printed or aired. Third, traditional media have taken to reporting those stories by quoting social media, rather than quoting social media's original sources. Fourth, by reporting stories that traditional media outlets would not, social media takes a niche-oriented strategy of attracting a smaller and more loyal audience. Fifth, young citizens do not shift their opinion in accordance with what the traditional media reports but rather are driven more by opinions and arguments shared via social media.[15] Social media users in South Korea tend to follow people they like, who express similar opinions and hold similar values with them. They demonstrate a very low rate of acceptance of different opinions, due to a strong tendency of self-oriented use of social media. Social media users apply very self-oriented standards in choosing their friends and following others.[16]

It is indicated that only 58.8 percent of Twitter accounts and 78.4 percent of Facebook accounts are registered with real names, which allows irresponsible leaks and immediately facilitates the spread of unconfirmed rumors. Some 71 percent of Twitter messages fail to be retweeted. Of the remainder, 92.42 percent are retweeted within one hour.[17]

The decline of the Cold War paradigm on the one hand and the threat perception generated by continued provocation by North Korea on the other have made South Korea's public opinion of North Korea split and become less predictable. The change was accompanied by the spread of the internet and social media, which enlarged citizen involvement in national security dialogue.

In the 2000s, national security is discussed in different cultural contexts, often with competing frames. The post–Cold War dominant discourse in South Korea has been formed by ideas and transnational values introduced by international non-governmental organizations and global media outlets. The new dominant discourse competes with the collective memory of the Korean War and the worst-case fears citizens are reminded of by repeated North Korean provocations.[18]

Briefings and information provided by the government are challenged by non-expert netizens who post, blog and tweet their opinions in cyberspace. This is how such issues as the sinking of ROKS *Cheonan*, the shelling of Yeonpyeong Island, the import of U.S. beef and the FTA with the United States have ignited ideological cleavages in public opinion. Due to unconfirmed stories spread via social media, the threat perception of the public is now vulnerable to manipulation by being exposed to confusing and inconsistent signals.[19] Sympathy over starvation in North Korea is not dulled by Pyongyang's nuclear tests. Community grievances and anger toward U.S. military personnel crimes, environmental pollution around U.S. bases and trade pressure from the United States are expressed in the midst of the shelling of Yeonpyeong Island. When Kim Jong-il died, the South Korean public was enraged by the killing of a maritime police officer by Chinese fishermen and the Japanese request to remove the statue of a Korean comfort woman in front of the Japanese Embassy in Seoul.

The sinking of ROKS *Cheonan* prompted conflicts with competing frames, which will be discussed later. Memories of the Korean War, as well as North Korean provocations on the one hand and memories of excessive classification of secrets and abuse of power by authoritarian military regimes on the other, are used respectively by conservative groups and liberal activists to solidify existing cultural repertories grounded in public dispositions.[20]

In the absence of substantiated evidence, it is not uncommon that unconfirmed rumors attract public attention. The government's abstaining from releasing sensitive military secrets also contributes to the spread of unrooted rumors. Unconfirmed stories spread by social media earn influence at the initial stage and recede over time. Then, rumors are gradually replaced by substantial analysis based on real facts reported by conventional media outlets. Likewise, the marginal influence of prominent bloggers and tweeters also declines, probably faster than the influence of objective coverage based on hard and real evidence.[21] However, the influence of some bloggers and tweeters remains intact, only to increase skepticism about official government announcements like what happened in the sinking of ROKS *Cheonan*.

Several reasons may be found why unconfirmed rumors are generated, which open more space for social media to insert its independent influence in its coverage of security affairs.[22]

First, the South Korean public has witnessed many cases in which public discontent over domestic issues is diffused by external crises which were known solely by government release.[23]

Second, little time is allowed for public discussion over how to respond to North Korean provocations. The decision to respond to North Korea's provocations should be carried out immediately on the spot, so that the conflict cannot be enlarged into a full-scale war. The immediacy offers little time for open discussion, which ignites belated debate regarding the responsibility of who did wrong and why it happened.

Third, ambivalence exists in the public mind on North Korea. During the Cold War period, confrontation with North Korea formed a dominant paradigm that generated a meta-schema that determined elite discourse, media coverage and public opinion on security affairs.[24] But this is no longer the case. Now, South Korean presidents have been put under the pressure of exercising patience in developing dialogue with North Korea while responding with resolute will to any provocation by Pyongyang. With North Korea as a constant threat, the global post–Cold War atmosphere and domestic democratization have made invoking patriotism and anti-communism to silence opposition more and more difficult.

Fourth, group psychology in the network makes one believe that he or she is supported by many in the group, although she or he cannot identify who they are and how many are there. Group psychology also generates in-group alignment and out-group expulsion, which furthers biased cognition of incoming data.[25]

Contrary to the dichotomy of capitalism and communism,

democracy and tyranny, and good and bad, the post–Cold War North Korea projects dual images of dialogue partner and provocateur, which requires a complicated array of words to explain South Korea's policy toward its northern counterpart. What decision makers want is not visual information that horrifies the public. Rather, they want media coverage with detailed contextual information so that public horror and disapproving majorities do not limit their ability to promote their policy alternatives. The reality shows an outflow of episodic frames wrapped with horrific images. Instead, we often witness variation between editorials and straight news, which is described as a "divorce" between factual discourse and misleading contents. The variation sends confusing signals which leave the readers in between reporters in the front who are tied to the daily pressure of covering ongoing events quickly and editorial editors on the desk who maintain a consistent one-step-back stance without regard to what is going on in the real world.[26]

Public and political messages have more chances to be tweeted. Users with a liberal political orientation occupy the majority among social media users, and they tend to deal more with political issues than others. In social media, emotions of anger and grief trigger more responses than joy and happiness.[27]

The influence of social media on North Korea has increased as the role of social media as a news source has increased. It is indicated that the percentage using social media as a source of news in South Korea increased from 11.4 percent in 2011 to 20.7 percent in 2014.

The frequency of social media usage also increased. The number of those who use social media on a daily basis for getting news increased from 2.8 percent in 2011 to 8.6 percent in 2014. However, the following table implies that the majority of citizens do not depend on social media as their daily source of news and information. Almost 80 percent of respondents did not use social media as their source for news information.

The number of social media users as of 2014 already exceeded the number of newspaper readers. According to a poll conducted

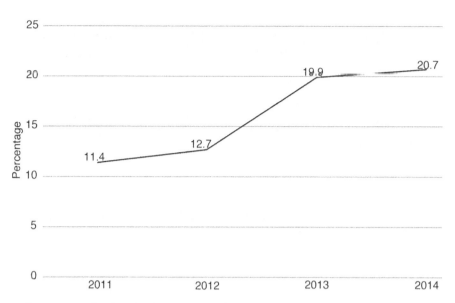

Figure 5–1: Tendencies in the Rate of News via Social Media Usage (2011 to 2014). 2011–2012 n=5,000, 2013 n=5,082, 2014 n=5,061. *Source: Korea Press Foundation,* Survey on Media Recipients' Recognition in 2014 *(December), p. 109.*

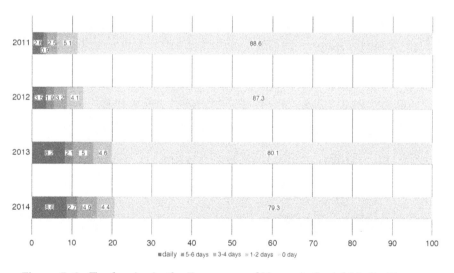

Figure 5–2: Tendencies in the Frequency of News via Social Media Usage (weekly basis/2011 to 2014). 2011–2012 n=5,000, 2013 n=5,082, 2014 n=5,061. *Source: Korea Press Foundation,* Survey on Media Recipients' Recognition in 2014, *p. 110.*

by the Korea Press Foundation, almost 50 percent of the respondents answered that they use social media.

TABLE 5–1: RATES OF USAGE TIME BY MEDIA TYPE (DECEMBER 2014)

| Type/ Measured Item | Number of Media Users (n) | Rate of Using Media (%) | Daily Media Using Rate (%) | Average Time of Using Media per day (min.) | |
|---|---|---|---|---|---|
| | | | | All Respondents | User Respondents by Media |
| TV | 4,775 | 94.4 | 75.4 | 166.5 | 176.4 |
| Internet (A+B) | 3,796 | 75.0 | | 166.8 | |
| Fixed Internet (A) | 3,517 | 69.5 | 54.7 | 60.2 | 86.6 |
| Mobile Internet (B) | 2,927 | 57.8 | 28.5 | 56.6 | 97.8 |
| Social Media | 2,527 | 49.9 | 35.1 | 22.1 | 44.3 |
| Newspaper | 1,555 | 30.7 | 7.4 | 10.4 | 33.8 |
| Radio | 1,182 | 23.4 | 8.7 | 23.0 | 98.3 |
| Magazine | 267 | 5.3 | 0.3 | 1.1 | 20.5 |

Source: http://www.kpf.or.kr/board/Z/detail.do?menu_link=pds/MediaStatsInfomation/ MediaStatsInfomation_04/summary&p_menu_id=null&menu_id=202&menu_orderby= 5&tabYn=N

Social media appear to be two times more influential than printed newspapers and one-eighth as influential as television. In 2014, respondents spent an average of 166.5 minutes a day watching television and 116.8 minutes using the internet, personal computers and mobile devices combined. They spent about 23 minutes listening to the radio and 22.1 minutes using social media. In terms of time, television is far more influential than social media because only one-eighth as much time is spent using social media as is spent watching television. What is more notable is that the time spent reading newspapers is only 10.4 minutes a day, implying that social media is two times more influential than newspapers.

TABLE 5–2: AVERAGE AMOUNT OF MEDIA USAGE TIME PER DAY (MIN.)

| Type/ Year | 1993 | 1996 | 1998 | 2000 | 2002 | 2004 | 2006 | 2008 | 2010 | 2011 | 2012 | 2013 | 2014 |
|---|---|---|---|---|---|---|---|---|---|---|---|---|---|
| TV | | 172.0 | 193.6 | 174.1 | 163.7 | 155.2 | 203.3 | 189.8 | 168.7 | 172.6 | 170.7 | 176.9 | 166.5 |
| Internet (A+B) | | | | | 77.0 | 67.1 | 90.7 | 82.0 | 85.3 | 108.7 | 108.6 | 116.3 | 116.8 |

| Type/ Year | 1993 | 1996 | 1998 | 2000 | 2002 | 2004 | 2006 | 2008 | 2010 | 2011 | 2012 | 2013 | 2014 |
|---|---|---|---|---|---|---|---|---|---|---|---|---|---|
| Fixed Internet (A) | | | | 77.0 | 67.1 | 90.7 | 82.0 | 69.2 | 79.2 | 67.2 | 62.6 | 60.2 | |
| Mobile Internet (B) | | | | | | | | | 16.1 | 29.5 | 41.4 | 53.7 | 56.6 |
| Radio | | | 66.3 | 61.2 | 70.8 | 43.6 | 37.0 | 40.4 | 29.0 | 34.9 | 26.0 | 26.8 | 23.0 |
| Social Media | | | | | | | | | | | | 25.3 | 22.1 |
| News-paper | 42.8 | 43.5 | 40.8 | 35.1 | 37.3 | 34.3 | 25.1 | 24.0 | 13.0 | 17.5 | 15.7 | 12.0 | 10.4 |
| Maga-zine | | | 7.6 | 10.5 | 13.0 | 9.0 | 6.2 | 4.9 | 5.4 | 3.6 | 2.6 | 2.3 | 1.1 |

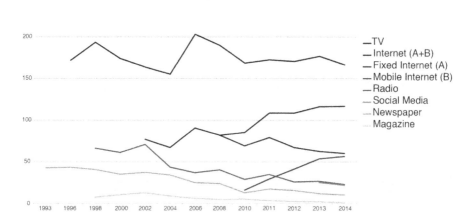

Figure 5–3: Average Media Usage Time by Media Type Per Day (min.)

In terms of time spent on getting news, however, social media appears less influential than printed newspapers. Out of 22.1 minutes for social media, 3.9 minutes are used for getting news, while all 10.4 minutes of reading a newspaper are used entirely for getting news. Of the 166.5 minutes for watching TV, 46.2 minutes are for watching TV news and current affairs programs, while 30.2 minutes out of 116.8 minutes spent using the internet are used for getting news information.

TABLE 5–3: AVERAGE TIME USING NEWS AND REPORTS
ON CURRENT AFFAIRS BY MEDIA TYPE (MIN.)

| Type/Year | 2010 | 2011 | 2012 | 2013 | 2014 |
|---|---|---|---|---|---|
| TV | 41.2 | 52.3 | 55.3 | 56.5 | 46.2 |
| Internet (A+B) | 15.5 | 29.9 | 32.7 | 30.3 | 30.2 |
| Fixed Internet (A) | 13.9 | 23.1 | 19.1 | 16.0 | 16.7 |
| Mobile Internet (B) | 1.6 | 6.8 | 13.6 | 14.3 | 13.5 |
| Newspaper | 13.0 | 17.5 | 15.7 | 12.0 | 10.4 |
| Radio | 5.4 | 8.8 | 6.0 | 6.0 | 4.4 |
| Social Media | | | | 4.2 | 3.9 |
| Magazine | 0.8 | 0.8 | 0.8 | 0.7 | 0.2 |

*2004–2006 n=1,200, 2008–2012 n=5,000, 2013 n=5,082, 2014 n=5,061

Source: http://www.kpf.or.kr/board/Z/detail.do?menu_link=pds/ MediaStatsInfomation/MediaStatsInfomation_04/summary&p_menu_ id=null&menu_id=202&menu_orderby=5&tabYn=N

Media users in South Korea tend to trust TV news the most and social media the least. Out of the scale of 0 to 5, respondents' trust on TV news was 3.9 versus 3.1 for news obtained from social media.

TABLE 5–4: RELIABILITY OF NEWS AND REPORTS ON
CURRENT AFFAIRS BY MEDIA TYPE (MEAN OF 5-POINT SCALE
FROM 1, ABSOLUTELY LOW, TO 5, ABSOLUTELY HIGH)

| Type/Year | 2010 (n=5,000) | 2011 (n=5,000) | 2012 (n=5,000) | 2013 (n=5,082) | 2014 (n=5,061) |
|---|---|---|---|---|---|
| Terrestrial Broadcasting | 4.04 | 3.83 | 3.76 | 4.13 | 3.90 |
| News Channel | 3.90 | 3.69 | 3.61 | 3.84 | 3.70 |
| Comprehensive Channel | | | 3.43 | 3.72 | 3.60 |
| National Newspaper | 3.79 | 3.44 | 3.37 | 3.65 | 3.43 |
| News Correspondent | | | | 3.61 | 3.47 |
| Portal Site News Service | | | | 3.58 | 3.50 |
| Economic (finance, business) Newspaper | | | | 3.48 | 3.45 |
| Radio | 3.60 | 3.54 | 3.41 | 3.47 | 3.42 |
| Local Daily Newspaper | 3.55 | 3.31 | 3.23 | 3.34 | 3.27 |
| Website of News Company | 3.49 | 3.28 | 3.16 | 3.23 | 3.14 |
| Internet Newspaper | 3.46 | 3.28 | 3.18 | 3.23 | 3.14 |
| Local Weekly Newspaper | 3.36 | 3.23 | 3.13 | 3.21 | 3.19 |

## 5.  Social Media and National Security

| Type/Year | 2010 (n=5,000) | 2011 (n=5,000) | 2012 (n=5,000) | 2013 (n=5,082) | 2014 (n=5,061) |
|---|---|---|---|---|---|
| Current Affairs Magazine | 3.48 | 3.28 | 3.14 | 3.17 | 3.16 |
| Social Media | | | | 3.15 | 3.10 |
| Media-Wide | | | 3.26 | 3.40 | 3.28 |

*Source: http://www.kpf.or.kr/board/Z/detail.do?menu_link=pds/MediaStatsInfoma-tion/MediaStatsInfomation_04/summary&p_menu_id=null&menu_id=202&menu_orde rby=5&tabYn=N*

Portal news appears to be far more influential than social media news. Some 88.5 percent of 3,394 respondents answered that they get news by clicking news titles from the main page of a portal site, while 30.8 percent answered they get news from social media.

### TABLE 5–5: SURVEY ON HOW TO USE INTERNET NEWS (MULTIPLE ANSWERS)

| No. | Selected Answers/Year | 2012 (%) | 2013 (%) | 2014 (%) |
|---|---|---|---|---|
| 1 | Click news after seeing the titles on the main page of portal sites | 87.4 | 71.5 | 88.5 |
| 2 | Search people or events on real-time search | 57.3 | 48.5 | 75.3 |
| 3 | Find out interesting fields or topics on news category in portal sites | 46.8 | 33.5 | 57.6 |
| 4 | Via social media | 12.5 | 30.4 | 30.8 |
| 5 | In the process of searching needed information | 40.5 | 29.5 | 62.1 |
| 6 | Type the interesting news in the search box | 29.4 | 23.1 | 49.7 |
| 7 | Via news applications | 18.2 | 15.9 | 18.7 |
| 8 | Search news of specific media company on news category in portal sites | 16.1 | 9.1 | 21.2 |
| 9 | Visit news company websites | 14.6 | 7.4 | 13 |
| 10 | Visit internet newspaper sites | 13.5 | 5.1 | 11 |
| 11 | Via "My Registered News" platform (my news, subscribe service, etc.) | 2.6 | 1.7 | 6.5 |
| 12 | E-mail newsletters | 2.3 | 1.1 | 5.9 |

(2012 n=3,129, 2013 n=3,324, 2014 n=3,394)

*Source: http://www.kpf.or.kr/board/Z/detail.do?menu_link=pds/Media StatsInfomation/MediaStatsInfomation_04/summary&p_menu_id=null& menu_id=202&menu_orderby=5&tabYn=N*

# 6

# Case Studies
# on Media Coverage
# and Influence

It is not common to find that major newspapers, TV news and social media employ contrasting frames. In general, media coverage of social protests or demonstrations tends to spotlight violent and abnormal aspects, thus framing them as social deviance by stressing illegitimacy and overemphasizing negative effects.[1] To the contrary, some TV news and social media coverage of the candlelight demonstrations in Seoul in 2002 and 2008 favorably framed anti–American demonstrations by emphasizing through the broadcasted images the peaceful character of the demonstrations. They portrayed the participants as ordinary citizens, students, housewives and children with their parents, all holding candles. Under the caption of "For Whom does the Police Exist?" they focused on the bleeding protesters that were hit by police clubs. This differed from the portrayal in the major newspapers, which highlighted protesters' violence directed at the police, thereby portraying the police as the defenders of mainstream society and the protesters as the offenders. The major press news maintained a conservative stance and positively evaluated U.S. security and economic roles on the peninsula.

The contrast implies that the frames used by TV news, major newspapers and social media were constructed by contrasting thematic frames that competed for dominance in the public domain: national interest on the one hand and national prestige and human interests on the other.[2] In this chapter, differences in frames between media outlets is the main topic. Then, the discussion moves on to the sources of contrast by scrutinizing differences between major TV networks and newspaper companies. Plausible explanations are provided when the differences in ownership and dependence on advertisement sponsors between TV news and major newspapers are put into consideration. In addition, media-politics links also provide important indicators as to why TV news and newspapers, by framing candlelight demonstrations, actively competed for influence over agenda setting. Lastly, social media exerts indispensable influence through postings by power bloggers and portal news, including some internet broadcastings that were retweeted and covered by the traditional media outlets. Questions for evaluating frames used by media outlets are summarized in Table 6–1.

### TABLE 6–1: FRAMES AND CHECKING POINTS

| Frames | Checking Points in the Story |
| --- | --- |
| National Interest | Mentions security/economic interests, calls for abstaining from emotional reactions, reports on decrease of numbers of demonstrators, pictures/scenes of demonstrators' violence and/or hardships experienced by police |
| National Prestige | Mentions inequality in U.S.–South Korean security/ trade relations, calls for South Korea's exercise of judicial/ quarantine authority, mentions crimes by U.S. soldiers/ environmental pollutions caused by U.S. forces in South Korea, mentions beef consumed in the United States is from cattle aged 24 months or younger or amending Status of Forces Agreement/renegotiation over beef imports |
| Human Interest | Mentions victims' school days, childhood photos, friends or family members, mentions people's concern about death by mad cow disease, offers expressions that stimulate personal hatred, feelings of victimization, anger, sympathy, fear of mad cow disease, concern over U.S. beef consumed for school and military meals |
| Domestic Politics | Mentions domestic political issues/elections, offers photo/scenes spotlighting non-violent character of candlelight demonstrations, gives descriptions of demonstrators as normal civilians or young students, |

**111**

| Frames | Checking Points in the Story |
|---|---|
| | correlates demonstrations with past democratic events such as June 10, 1987, demonstrations, 2002 candlelight demonstrations, 2002 World Cup soccer, or resignation of president |
| Responsibility | Mentions the South Korean government's responsibility to the U.S. government, any solution such as a priori notice of training exercises and movements of armored vehicles, amendments of the SOFA, renegotiation over the import of U.S. beef or FTA, responsibility to individuals |
| Conflict | Mentions differing views or positions or lack of cooperation between the United States and South Korean government bureaus in charge, offers criticisms or attribution of responsibility calling for apology from the United States, political slogans or description of behavior that express anti-Americanism, or any photo displaying such content(s), highlights domestic conflicts between conservatives and liberals |
| Economic Effect | Mentions economic effects caused by North Korea's provocations, worsened inter–Korean relations, economic sanctions, stock market fluctuations, purchase of emergency food, financial damages of companies in Kaesong Industrial Complex |

## Anti-Americanism

Here, we analyze three cases of media influence on anti–Americanism in South Korea: the candlelight demonstrations in 2002 over the deaths of two female middle-school students killed by a 50-ton Bradley armored vehicle of the U.S. Second Division during a military exercise on a narrow road north of Seoul; mass demonstrations in 2008 against the import of U.S. beef; and the signing of the U.S.–South Korean Free Trade Agreement (FTA).

In South Korea, the main source of anti–Americanism was the alleged American involvement in the redeployment of South Korean troops for suppressing the Gwangju Uprising in 1980. In May 1980, the U.S. military command in South Korea allegedly acquiesced to release South Korean troops from U.S. operational control for redeployment in Gwangju, and these troops killed hundreds of antigovernment protesters.[3] This changed the perception of the United States from a fraternal alliance partner to a two-faced interferer who supported an authoritarian military general who suppressed democracy.

Another source of anti–Americanism is economic pressure to open up South Korean markets for U.S. beef and grain. As soon as South Korea achieved a trade surplus with the United States in the mid–1980s, Washington demanded greater market access for U.S. agricultural product and capital goods. In particular, opening the rice market provoked nationalist sentiment because it was "perceived as an assault on Korea's pride."[4]

The rise of anti–Americanism is also related to the change in demographic structure in South Korea. As the Korean War generation aged and the democratic movement generation emerged as the leading group of the society, the United States came to be perceived more and more as an antidemocratic supporter of the authoritarian regime and as the symbol of economic pressure. At the same time, the image of America as an alliance partner in the Korean War gradually weakened.[5] Although anti–Americanism had been a hallmark of student activists and progressive leaders since the 1980s, for most citizens, the U.S.–South Korean alliance had been a forbidden subject, and its unequal and asymmetric aspects were not to be engaged with. In accordance, the media had tended to zoom in on violence in their coverage of anti–American protests, physical fights with the police, Molotov cocktails, destruction of public facilities and illegal infiltration into U.S. facilities. These behaviors may be interpreted as threats to public order. The same thing was true in the American media's coverage of anti–Vietnam War protests in which Viet Cong flags and communist elements were intentionally highlighted and exaggerated.[6]

As democratization developed in the early 1990s, the conservatives gradually lost control of public agenda setting over anti–Americanism. Democratization opened the way for the public to step into the discussion on security affairs, mostly on relations with North Korea and the United States. As various civil movement organizations registered their own views over security issues including U.S.–South Korean relations, anti–American complaints bridged political standpoints and ideological gaps between civil movement organizations in South Korea.[7] The public began to express community grievances and anger toward the U.S. troops in cases of U.S. military personnel crimes and environmental pollution around U.S. bases and their firing ranges. In particular, the South Korean public reacted very sensitively toward sexual crimes with female victims, as in the case of the brutal murder of Yun Geumi, who became the symbol of South Korea's "powerlessness and victimization by the United States."[8]

Against this backdrop, this study examines three frames for analyzing anti–Americanism: national interest, national prestige and human interest.[9] First, as we have already mentioned, anti–Americanism functions as a useful tool for eliciting popular support.[10] In South Korea, too, anti–Americanism has been a hot potato in the debates between conservatives and progressives[11] since the 1980s. Conservative emphasis on security and economic interest was contrasted with progressive emphasis on national prestige and human interest. Under military regimes, stories on crimes committed by U.S. soldiers with female victims and environmental problems surrounding U.S. bases received low-key attention, due to U.S. contribution in terms of security against military threats from North Korea. As the process of democratization triggered more calls for equal relations with the United States, national prestige and human interest attracted more attention than national security.

On June 13, 2002, two female eighth-grade students were crushed by a Bradley armored vehicle moving along a narrow local road in Yangju County, north of Seoul, during a training exercise by the U.S. Second Infantry Division. The case was brought before a U.S. court-martial, in accordance with the SOFA that stipulates

U.S. judicial authority over accidents during official operations. Two U.S. soldiers, the commander of the armored vehicle and the driver were subsequently court-martialed on charges of negligent homicide. The prosecutor asserted that the two servicemen had had sufficient time to prevent the accident. The focal point of the court was whether the driver heard a warning to stop before running down the girls. If convicted, the commander and driver could have faced a prison term of up to six years. For their part, the South Korean public called for their government's exercise of the judicial right to detain the two U.S. soldiers and for the amendment of the SOFA, labeling it as a nonequal treaty. It was indicated that the South Korean government could exercise judicial authorities over only 7 percent of the crimes committed by U.S. soldiers on the peninsula.

The two soldiers were acquitted of negligent homicide charges on November 20 and 22, thereby prompting furious responses from anti–American activist groups, which prompted the slogan of "two girls dead and no one guilty." The civil movement activists asserted that the accident was in fact avoidable and that the two soldiers had neglected their duty of care. The difference in the legal systems of South Korea and the United States was also a factor that further agitated the South Korean public. Unlike in the United States, South Korean prosecutors are permitted to appeal a not-guilty verdict. Thus, the South Korean public was angered at the release of the two soldiers because, had the case been under the South Korean judicial system's authority, they could have still faced prosecution. The not-guilty verdict triggered negative responses within the media. For example, MBC asserted that a guilty verdict had been impossible from the beginning, when the case was heard in a court composed of only U.S. servicemen with little will to prosecute the soldiers.[12] Two days later when the driver was found not guilty, the same news media spelled out the phrase "a court of two victims with no suspects."[13] The anti–American sentiment ultimately brought about nationwide candlelight demonstrations which mobilized roughly more than a million citizens.

In May 2008, anti–American candlelight demonstrations were again held in order to call for the ban of the importation of U.S. beef from cattle aged 30 months or older, which could in theory cause mad cow disease. The U.S.–South Korean agreement on South Korea's import of U.S. beef was portrayed as the de facto opening of South Korea's beef market and as President Lee Myung-bak's gift to President George W. Bush at the U.S.–South Korean summit held at Camp David in April. The demonstrations developed into a domestic political issue as demonstrators called for Lee's apology and, in some cases, resignation.

U.S. beef has been a political football since South Korea banned its import on December 27, 2003, following a case in the state of Washington of mad cow disease, a fatal brain illness that might be transmitted to humans. Despite U.S. efforts to reopen its third-largest overseas market for American beef, with imports totaling $800 million a year, the resumption of South Korea's import of U.S. beef was suspended as another mad cow case was found in June 2005.

Thereafter, a cycle of imposing and lifting the ban was repeated. Through a series of negotiations between Seoul and Washington, South Korea lifted its ban of U.S. beef imports, which had lasted for two years and ten months. On October 30, 2006, South Korea imported nine tons of U.S. beef. However, all nine tons of beef were returned to the United States because the South Korean quarantine found a piece of bone which might have contained SRM (Specified Risk Materials) that might cause mad cow disease. In April 2007, 6.4 tons of U.S. beef were imported after high-level negotiations the previous month on the quarantine of livestock products.. However, after pieces of ribs and spinal cords were found repeatedly in May, August and October, South Korea's quarantine authority decided to reship the beef back to the United States. In October, South Korea agreed to import U.S. beef ribs, one of the most popular beef parts in the country, although no solid agreement was reached.

It was in April 2008 that the newly inaugurated president, Lee Myung-bak, lifted a five-year-old ban on American beef imports, thereby allowing U.S. exporters to ship beef from all cattle without restriction on age. Lee encountered a public furor over his "yielding" deal with the United States, being accused of ignoring the health risks to his citizens. An MBC program, *Producer's Notepad,* carried a story on mad cow disease and set off massive demonstrations. Demonstrators asked for there to be a renegotiation with the United States and called for restricting beef imports to cattle less than 30 months old. Younger cattle are considered to pose less risk of mad cow disease.

As demonstrators gradually expressed grievances over other policies initiated by the Lee government, candlelight demonstrations snowballed into antigovernment protests calling for "Lee out!" Lee's approval ratings dipped below 20 percent. Lee had to replace nine of ten senior Blue House staff in the hope that doing so would quell public furor over the unpopular deal on U.S. beef imports. In August, Lee also replaced his minister for food, agriculture, forestry and fisheries, who was in charge of the negotiations over U.S. beef imports. It required further observation as to whether several restrictions would be lifted, such as restrictions of U.S. beef exports to South Korea of cattle 30 months old or younger and the import of cattle parts such as brains, eyes, skulls and spinal cords, which many Koreans believe to carry mad cow disease.

Lastly, the U.S.–South Korean Free Trade Agreement also triggered nationwide anti–American demonstrations. The negotiations started as early as 2006 and seemed to be concluded when both sides signed the agreement in 2007. The agreement encountered opposition from both sides. United Automobile Workers, an American labor union for American and Canadian workers in the automobile industry, called for balanced car trade between the United States and South Korea. In 2010, the number of South Korea's automobile exports to the United States was about 513,000, while it imported about 7,450 U.S. cars. For their part, South Korean filmmakers called for more quotas for domestic films, and the livestock industry called for continued protection. Since mistranslation of the signed agreement generated serious controversy at the last stage of ratification in May 2011, the process triggered numerous postings on online discussion websites. In November, ratification failed at the National Assembly, and one of the leading members, Chung Dong-young, carried out a protest outside the National Assembly building. Massive rallies took place in December, and the South Korean government announced a $2.5 billion additional budget to compensate for financial damages caused by the FTA. Even after the U.S.–South Korean FTA went into effect in March 2012, the number of online postings did not decrease, exerting continued influence on the FTA issues.

Major TV news, newspapers and social media employed frames in their coverage of the candlelight demonstrations in 2002 and 2008 and the process of the U.S.–South Korean Free Trade Agreement (FTA). For this, this chapter of the book analyzes 1,101 TV and press news stories released between June 13, 2002, and January 5, 2003, and 927 TV and press news stories released between May 3 and June 20, 2008. In addition, this study analyzes trends in the number of independent internet broadcasts and postings over the 2008 candlelight demonstrations and the FTA signing.

For the 2002 case, most stories were released after November 18, when the U.S. military authority held the court-martial. The number of articles dropped significantly after January 5, 2003, as the overall attention of the society was shifted to the president-elect, Roh Moo-hyun, who called for abstaining from anti–American demonstrations. For the 2008 case, the candlelight demonstrations snowballed from May in terms of the number of participants. However, the number decreased as the government moved to renegotiate with the United States over the import of beef cattle older than 30 months. Stories from prime-time news on KBS, MBC and SBS, three nationwide TV networks, and from the *Chosun Ilbo*, *Joongang Ilbo* and *Donga Ilbo* newspapers have been selected for

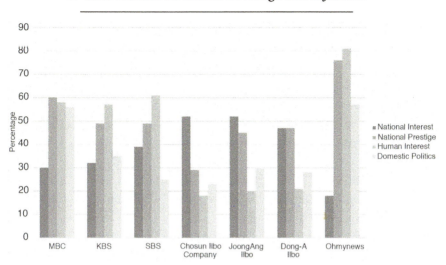

Figure 6–1: Frames of Media Coverage: 2002 Accident. Modified from Yongho Kim and Jaeyoung Hur, "Framing Anti-Americanism and the Media in South Korea: TV vs Newspaper," *Pacific Focus* 24:3 (2009), p. 350.

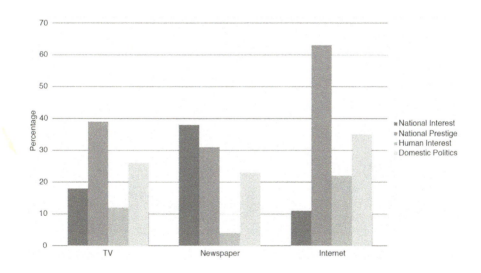

Figure 6–2: Comparison of Frames: 2002 Accident. Modified from Yongho Kim and Jaeyoung Hur, "Framing Anti-Americanism and the Media in South Korea: TV vs Newspaper," *Pacific Focus* 24:3 (2009), p. 350.

analysis based on circulation.[14] It is important to note that most stories were found to contain more than one frame.

In 2002, TV's rare use of the national interest frame contrasted with the newspapers' rare use of national prestige. In particular, news stories aired by MBC appeared to humanize the accident and to link the accident to the 2002 presidential election. To the contrary, newspapers abstained from using human-interest frames.

In 2008, TV news described the import of beef as the Lee Myung-bak government's "subservient" diplomacy toward the United States, while newspapers warned the progressive groups about using beef imports as political tools for destabilizing the Lee government. Again, newspapers' frequent use of national interest frames contrasted with the frequent use of national prestige frames by TV news. The trend of TV news to emphasize human interest continued. It indicated U.S. beef would be mostly used for school

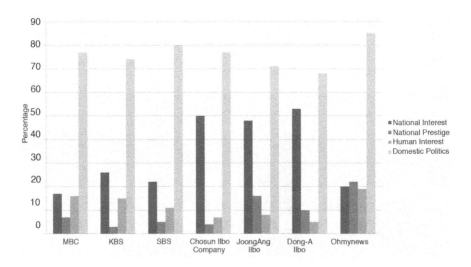

Figure 6–3: Frames of Media Company: 2008 Anti–U.S. Beef Import Demonstrations. Modified from Yongho Kim and Jaeyoung Hur, "Framing Anti-Americanism and the Media in South Korea: TV vs Newspaper," *Pacific Focus* 24:3 (2009), p. 351.

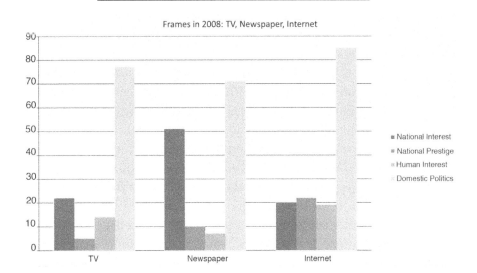

Figure 6–4: Comparison of Frames: 2008 Anti–U.S. Beef Import Demonstrations. Modified from Yongho Kim and Jaeyoung Hur, "Framing Anti-Americanism and the Media in South Korea: TV vs Newspaper," *Pacific Focus* 24:3 (2009), p. 352.

lunches and military meals and highlighted the reactions of students and mothers whose sons would soon be enlisted.

Analysis shows the stark difference of frames between newspapers and TV news. The frequency of the national interest frames that appeared in newspaper stories (38 percent in 2002 and 51 percent in 2008) was far larger than in TV news stories (19 percent in 2002 and 22 percent in 2008). In contrast, TV news stories contained the human interest frame more frequently (12 percent in 2002 and 14 percent in 2008) than did newspaper stories (5 percent in 2002 and 7 percent in 2008). As shown in Figures 1 and 3, some 37 percent (2002) and 50 percent (2008) of *Chosun Ilbo* stories, 42 percent (2002) and 48 percent (2008) of *Joongang Ilbo* stories and 35 percent (2002) and 53 percent (2008) of *Donga Ilbo* stories contained the national interest frame. In contrast, only 15 percent (2002) and 17 percent (2008) of MBC news stories, 22 percent

(2002) and 26 percent (2008) of KBS news stories, and 20 percent (2002) and 22 percent (2008) of SBS news stories carried the national interest frame.

Other contrasts were found in the usage of the national prestige and human interest frames. In 2002, some 40 percent of TV news used the national prestige frame, while 31 percent of newspaper stories contained this frame. It is also notable that in 2002 only 5 percent of newspaper stories used the human interest frame, while 12 percent of TV news stories used the frame. In 2008, some 7 percent of newspaper stories used the human interest frame, while 14 percent of TV news stories employed the frame.

The differences in using frames reflect the media companies' ideological colors. It is widely accepted that *Chosun Ilbo* occupies the conservative end, while *Hankyoreh* occupies the other extreme. *Hankyoreh's* coverage of the two candlelight demonstrations is notable in several perspectives. First, *Hankyoreh* carried more stories than

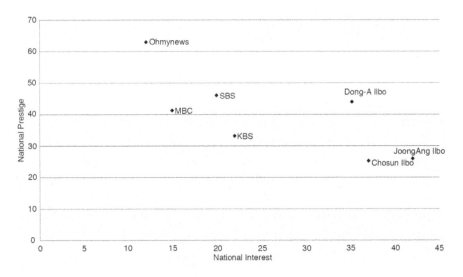

Figure 6–5: Comparison of Media Companies: National Interest vs. National Prestige (2002). Modified from Yongho Kim and Jaeyoung Hur, "Framing Anti-Americanism and the Media in South Korea: TV vs Newspaper," *Pacific Focus* 24:3 (2009), p. 352.

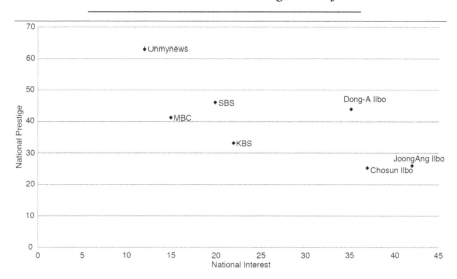

Figure 6–6: Comparison of Media Companies: National Interest vs. Human Interest (2002). Modified from Yongho Kim and Jaeyoung Hur, "Framing Anti-Americanism and the Media in South Korea: TV vs Newspaper," *Pacific Focus* 24:3 (2009), p. 353.

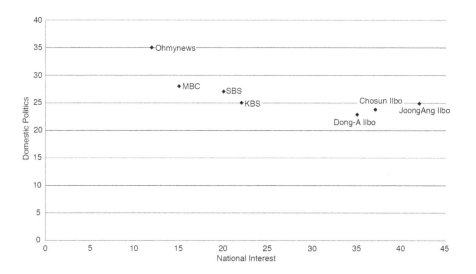

Figure 6–7: Comparison of Media Companies: National Interest vs. Domestic Politics (2002)

major newspapers did. It published 299 stories in 2002 and 235 stories in 2008, more than *Chosun* (169 in 2002 and 102 in 2008), *Joongang* (143 in 2002 and 125 in 2008) and *Donga* (134 in 2002 and 161 in 2008). Second, *Hankyoreh* focused on police violence in suppressing the demonstrations and at the same time highlighted peaceful aspects of the demonstrations.[15] Third, *Hankyoreh* criticized major newspapers' coverage of the candlelight demonstrations.[16] Fourth, *Hankyoreh* launched several series of articles criticizing the U.S. forces in South Korea in 2002[17] and 2008, criticizing the overall policy pursued by the Lee Myung-bak government.[18] Nevertheless, this analysis excluded *Hankyoreh* because it publishes 500,000 papers a day,[19] while the three major newspapers publish more than two million papers daily, as mentioned in footnote 26. This implies that *Hankyoreh's* influence on ordinary readers is relatively limited compared with the major newspapers, regardless of its importance in South Korea's media world.

In this analysis, *Chosun Ilbo* and MBC occupy the conservative and progressive extremes. In 2002, *Chosun Ilbo's* rare use of the national prestige frame (25 percent) and human interest frame (4 percent) may be interpreted as its conservative character in trying to avoid correlating the accident with anti–Americanism. In contrast, MBC's heavy dependence on national prestige (41 percent) and human interest (15 percent) marked an obvious variation from other media news. In 2008, *Chosun Ilbo,* along with *Joongang Ilbo* and *Donga Ilbo,* used the national interest frame frequently to illuminate that economic and trade relations with the United States should not be damaged by anti–Americanism. The newspaper also joined other major newspapers in reminding citizens that anti–American coverage by MBC was in fact a politically oriented domestic movement against the conservative Lee Myung-bak government.

An evaluation by a conservative media watchdog called Civil Coalition for Fairness in Media criticized the reports by KBS and MBC stating that they disproportionately allocated time ranging from 69.6 percent to 76.1 percent for setting out the risks of mad

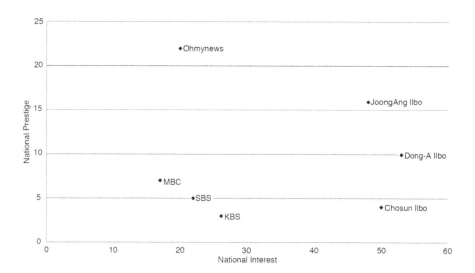

Figure 6–8: Comparison of Media Companies: National Interest vs. National Prestige (2008). Modified from Yongho Kim and Jaeyoung Hur, "Framing Anti-Americanism and the Media in South Korea: TV vs Newspaper," *Pacific Focus* 24:3 (2009), p. 354.

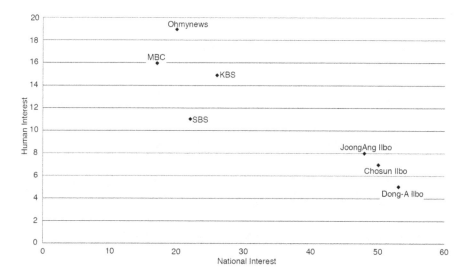

Figure 6–9: Comparison of Media Companies: National Interest vs. Human Interest (2008). Modified from Yongho Kim and Jaeyoung Hur, "Framing Anti-Americanism and the Media in South Korea: TV vs Newspaper," *Pacific Focus* 24:3 (2009), p. 355.

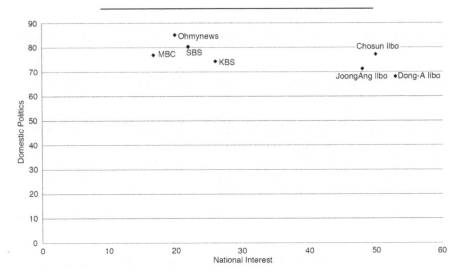

Figure 6–10: Comparison of Media Companies: National Interest vs. Domestic Politics (2008)

cow disease. For example, MBC's *PD's Notepad* on May 13, 2008, allocated 924 seconds (74.6 percent) for reporting a demonstrator's view of American beef containing SRM that could cause mad cow disease, while assigning 235 seconds (19 percent) for conveying the governmental position that American beef would be safe. According to this evaluation, other exemplary cases of news anchor remarks that allegedly triggered anti–American sentiment are: "(an) American official's explanation was long, but nothing new" (KBS); "the police became more violent in reacting to demonstrations" (MBC); "whether to renegotiate (over American beef imports) entirely depends on the government's will and time is running out" (MBC); "candlelight demonstrations are spreading like wildfire" (MBC); "Reporter doubts that our Agriculture Ministry takes care of business interests of American beef producers" (MBC); and "very bizarre combination of demonstrators from mothers with baby carts to reserve forces ... all over the city" (MBC).[20] After the release of the evaluation, MBC registered discontent over this evaluation and called for reevaluation by an ideologically neutral organization.

TV news also framed the accident in 2002 and the beef import in 2008 in ways to stimulate anti–Americanism by conveying visual messages dissimilar to text content. For example, on May 2, 2008, MBC's prime-time news program, *NewsDesk,* showed crippling and falling-down cows when it reported a government official's statement that "American beef is safe and human cow disease is disappearing." Likewise, the same program showed scenes of the anti–American candlelight demonstrations when it reported interdiction of a North Korean vessel by the Spanish navy in cooperation with the United States.[21] The vessel was heading toward Yemen with missiles on board.

On July 31, 2008, South Korea's Supreme Court ruled that MBC should run corrections to its report on the risks associated with American beef. Before this, the Ministry for Food, Agriculture and Fisheries had registered criticisms accusing MBC's program *PD's Notepad* of spreading unconfirmed risks of the brain-wasting disease on June 20. MBC filed an appeal of the court ruling.[22]

In addition, social media like independent internet TV broadcasts influenced anti–American demonstrations in 2008 by attracting a wide range of young viewers who knew how to post visual information and to access independent internet TV such as afreecaTV. The number of broadcasts uploaded on afreecaTV increased from 473 broadcasts to 2,501 broadcasts within a period of one week between May 25 and June 1, 2008. The number of views increased accordingly, from 240,000 view to 1,270,000 view within the same one-week period. On June 1, some 100,000 viewers watched the uploaded broadcasts simultaneously.[23] Stories and opinions uploaded to an internet debate forum called *Agora* and an online discussion website at *Daum,* one of the leading social portals in South Korea, were evaluated for their influence on South Korea's policy on U.S. beef imports. As demonstrated in Table 6–2, opinions posted on *Agora* started from nine stories on the day when the debate started, April 8, and marked almost 800 stories before the number began to decrease in October.

TABLE 6–2: OPINIONS AND STORIES UPLOADED ON AGORA

| Weeks | Opinions/ Stories | Weeks | Opinions/ Stories |
|---|---|---|---|
| April 8: Starting Day | 9 | July 12–25 | 775 |
| April 19–25: First Week | 131 | July 26–August 8 | 795 |
| April 26–May 2: Second Week | 577 | August 9–22 | 794 |
| May 3–16 | 794 | August 23–September 5 | 797 |
| May 17–30 | 796 | September 6–19 | 798 |
| May 31–June 13 | 789 | September 20–October 3 | 792 |
| June 14–June 27 | 789 | October 4–17 | 531 |
| June 28–July 11 | 772 | October 18–31 | 398 |

Source: Tae-Eun Song, "The Multitude's Foreign Policy Debates and Its Collective Behavior through Social Media: The Impact of Changing Communication Environment on the Public's Foreign Policy Attitudes," Korean Journal of International Relations 53:1 (2013), p. 60.

The anti–American demonstrations in 2008 marked the first case in which foreign issues were influenced by social media. Bilateral trade issues were discussed less in terms of national interests and more in terms of national prestige. In addition, slogans of "eating what Americans do not" were spreading fast through social media. The same was true over the FTA. Opinions and stories uploaded and tweeted in social media influenced the formation of negative public opinion on the agreement.

TABLE 6–3: NUMBER OF DISCUSSION POSTINGS ON RENEGOTIATION OF THE U.S.–SOUTH KOREAN FTA ON AGORA, ONLINE DISCUSSION WEBSITE AT DAUM, AND THE TIMELINE OF RENEGOTIATIONS OF U.S.–SOUTH KOREAN FTA (FROM DECEMBER 3, 2010, TO DECEMBER 31, 2012)

| Period | Number of Discussion Postings | Progress of Renegotiation |
|---|---|---|
| Dec. 3, 2010– Feb. 9, 2011 | 666 | Dec. 3, 2010: Reached negotiation of the FTA |
| Feb. 10– May 3, 2011 | 690 | Feb. 10, 2011: Signed and exchanged the accord renegotiation documents |

# 6. Case Studies on Media Coverage and Influence

| | Period | Number of Discussion Postings | Progress of Renegotiation |
|---|---|---|---|
| **Beginning of Serious Controversy (mistranslation of the negotiation agreement into Korean disclosed via media)** | May 4, 2011 | 18 | May 4, 2011: Withdrawal of the agreement by National Assembly Committee on Unification, Foreign Affairs and Trade due to the mistranslation of the document |
| **1 Month after the Disputes** | May 5– May 31, 2011 | 708 | |
| **2 Months after the Disputes** | June– June 30, 2011 | 665 | June 3, 2011: Presentation of the ratification bill on the FTA to the National Assembly |
| **3 Months after the Disputes** | July 1– July 31, 2011 | 630 | |
| **4 Months after the Disputes** | Aug. 1– Aug. 31, 2011 | 721 | |
| **5 Months after the Disputes** | Sept. 1– Sept. 30, 2011 | 768 | Sept. 16, 2011: Proposal of the bill to the National Assembly Committee on Unification, Foreign Affairs and Trade |
| **6 Months after the Disputes** | Oct. 1– Oct. 31, 2011 | 784 | Oct. 3, 2011: U.S. Congress submitted the FTA implementing legislation

Oct. 5, 2011: U.S. House of Representatives Ways and Means Committee passed the FTA implementation bill

Oct. 11, 2011: U.S. Senate Finance Committee passed the FTA implementation bill

Oct. 12, 2011: The FTA implementation bill |

## Social Media and South Korean National Security

| Period | Number of Discussion Postings | Progress of Renegotiation |
|---|---|---|
| | | passed at the plenary session of Congress |
| | | Oct. 21, 2011: U.S. president signed the FTA implementation bill |
| **7 Months after the Disputes** Nov. 1–Nov. 30, 2011 | 780 | Nov. 4, 2011: FTA failed to be ratified at the National Assembly |
| | | Nov. 22, 2011: FTA ratification bill passed at the National Assembly's plenary session |
| | | Nov. 25, 2011: Chung Dong-young, one of top members of Democratic Party, carried out the anti-FTA protest outside the National Assembly |
| | | Nov. 29, 2011: President Lee Myung-bak signed 14 implementation legislation bills of the FTA |
| **8 Months after the Disputes** Dec. 1–Dec. 31, 2011 | 785 | Dec. 3, 2011: Massive anti-FTA rallies occurred, followed by clashes with police |
| **9 Months after the Disputes** Jan. 1–Jan. 31, 2012 | 779 | Jan. 2, 2012: South Korean government announced the additional funding of 2.9 trillion won to compensate damages caused by FTA and strengthen competitiveness of the economy |
| **10 Months after the Disputes** Feb. 1–Feb. 29, 2012 | 775 | Feb. 21, 2012: Agreement reached on the |

| | Period | Number of Discussion Postings | Progress of Renegotiation |
|---|---|---|---|
| | | | effective date of the FTA |
| **11 Months after the Disputes** | March 1–March 31, 2012 | 784 | March 15, 2012: The FTA officially took effect |
| **1 Year after the Disputes** | Apr. 1–Apr. 30, 2012 | 785 | |
| **1 Year, 1 Month after the Disputes** | May 1–May 31, 2012 | 777 | May 15–18, 2012: A joint committee on the FTA held |
| **1 Year, 2 Months after the Disputes** | June 1–June 30, 2012 | 497 | June 7, 2012: ISD issue of the FTA was put on the discussion table in U.S. |
| **1 Year, 3 Months after the Disputes** | July 1–July 31, 2012 | 401 | July 5, 2012: Medicines and Medical Devices Committee of FTA held in Seoul |
| **1 Year, 4 Months after the Disputes** | Aug. 1–Aug. 31, 2012 | 318 | |
| **1 Year, 5 Months after the Disputes** | Sept. 1–Sept. 30, 2012 | 409 | |
| **1 Year, 6 Months after the Disputes** | Oct. 1–Oct. 31, 2012 | 402 | |
| **1 Year, 7 Months after the Disputes** | Nov. 1–Nov. 30, 2012 | 529 | Nov: 14, 2012: Regular trade meetings on the FTA held in Seoul; Nov. 28, 2012: Medicines and Medical Devices Committee of the FTA held in Washington, D.C. |
| **1 Year, 8 Months after the Disputes** | Dec. 1–Dec. 31, 2012 | 783 | Dec. 24, 2012: Protocol on Textile Rules of Origin within the FTA signed |

*Source: Tae-Eun Song, "The Multitude's Foreign Policy Debates and Its Collective Behavior through Social Media: The Impact of Changing Communication Environment on the Public's Foreign Policy Attitudes," Korean Journal of International Relations 53:1 (2013), pp. 65–66.*

Table 6–3 demonstrates how social media were active in the ratification process of the FTA from the concluding point of the negotiation to the ratification and its aftermath. Social media postings functioned as political pressure on assembly members, as the number of postings demonstrates. One month before the signed agreement was delivered to the National Assembly for ratification, the number of postings reached 721. It continued to stay above 700 up to two months after the FTA went into effect. The pressure led to the protest by one of the leading opposition members outside the assembly building in November.

## North Korean Missile and Nuclear Tests

In this section, we scrutinize media coverage of four cases of North Korean provocations that took place between the years 2006 and 2012: North Korea's missile test launch in 2006, the nuclear test in the same year, the test launch of a long-range missile in 2012 and the launch of Unha (Galaxy) 3 in the same year.

North Korea's test launch in 2006 represented its attempt to develop long-range rockets to deliver nuclear weapons, which Pyongyang had declared itself to be in possession of in the previous year. On July 5, 2006, North Korea test-fired seven missiles over the East Sea, including one intercontinental missile known as the Taepodong 2, which triggered international pressure to bring Pyongyang back to the six-party talks. The intercontinental missile, which according to the North Korean media was designed to target Alaska, was aborted roughly 40 seconds after the launch.[24]

Although the United States evaluated the test as a failure, there was growing concern that North Korean missiles with nuclear warheads could someday reach the soil of the United States by improving what went wrong in the series of test launches of liquid-fueled rockets. Other missile tests also generated concern in the international community because they were the short-range Scud-C-type missiles and medium-range Rodong missiles which North Korea has sold to Iran and Pakistan.

The test launch came in defiance of repeated warnings from the United States, Japan, South Korea and China. It came several minutes after the U.S. space shuttle *Discovery* was launched from Florida on Independence Day. Japan appeared more sensitive than it had to the previous launch in 1998, when North Korea's Tae-podong 1 flew over Japan before it fell into the Japanese sea, where several fishing boats were present. The launch was even more embarrassing to China, not only because China was not notified of the launch but also because it took place despite many official and public warnings by China. Up until several days before the test, China tried in vain to invite North Korea back to the six-party talks.

The launch prompted conservative opposition to "aid-pouring" policies and ignited an ideological confrontation embedded in South Korean society in the midst of almost ten years' pursuit of engagement with North Korea. Against this backdrop, a review of media coverage of the launch yields meaningful insights of media influence in security in the 2000s.

For this case, a total of 875 stories published between July 6 and July 16 were collected.

### TABLE 6–4: MEDIA COVERAGE OF NORTH KOREA'S MISSILE LAUNCH IN 2006

| Media | Number of stories |
|---|---|
| *Chosun Ilbo* | 158 |
| *Joongang Ilbo* | 139 |
| *Donga Ilbo* | 101 |
| *Hankyoreh Shinmun* | 122 |
| *Kyunghyang Shinmun* | 112 |
| KBS | 48 |
| MBC | 73 |
| SBS | 122 |
| TOTAL | 875 |

133

TABLE 6–5: NUMBER OF FRAMES (MULTI-CODING)

|  | Chosun Ilbo | Joon-gang Ilbo | Dong-a Ilbo | Hanky-oreh | Kyungh-yang Shinmun | KBS | MBC | SBS | Total |
|---|---|---|---|---|---|---|---|---|---|
| Conflict Frame | 158 | 168 | 102 | 171 | 186 | 80 | 106 | 195 | 1,166 |
| Responsibility Frame | 238 | 167 | 155 | 132 | 107 | 33 | 68 | 112 | 1,012 |
| Crisis Escalation Frame | 65 | 60 | 36 | 39 | 29 | 26 | 29 | 40 | 324 |
| Economic Effect Frame | 13 | 22 | 10 | 24 | 14 | 5 | 16 | 19 | 123 |
| TOTAL | 474 | 417 | 303 | 366 | 336 | 144 | 219 | 366 | 2,625 |

TABLE 6–6: PERCENTAGE OF FRAMES

|  | Chosun Ilbo | Joon-gang Ilbo | Dong-a Ilbo | Hanky-oreh | Kyungh-yang Shinmun | KBS | MBC | SBS | Aver-age |
|---|---|---|---|---|---|---|---|---|---|
| Conflict Frame | 33.3 | 40.3 | 33.7 | 46.7 | 55.4 | 55.6 | 48.4 | 53.3 | 44.4 |
| Responsibility Frame | 50.2 | 40.0 | 51.2 | 36.1 | 31.8 | 22.9 | 31.1 | 30.6 | 38.6 |
| Crisis Escalation Frame | 13.7 | 14.4 | 11.9 | 10.7 | 8.6 | 18.1 | 13.2 | 10.9 | 12.3 |
| Economic Effect Frame | 2.7 | 5.3 | 3.3 | 6.6 | 4.2 | 3.5 | 7.3 | 5.2 | 4.7 |
| TOTAL | 100.0 | 100.0 | 100.0 | 100.0 | 100.0 | 100.0 | 100.0 | 100.0 | 100.0 |

Frames used by conservative newspapers and by liberal newspapers demonstrated sharp contrasts. While conservative newspapers described the launch as a provocation by North Korea, liberal newspapers and TV news viewed the launch as the result of inter–Korean conflict. Conservative media tended to convey the message that Kim Jong-il was responsible and the launch was the result of North Korea's provocative policy. All media foresaw little negative impact on the South Korean economy and little possibility of tension escalation.

# The Nuclear Test in 2006

When North Korea conducted the nuclear test on October 8, 2006, the official media in North Korea, the Korea Central News Agency (KCNA) described the test as a "historic event" designed

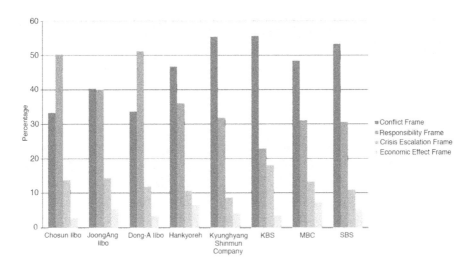

Figure 6–11: North Korea's Test Launch of Missiles in 2006

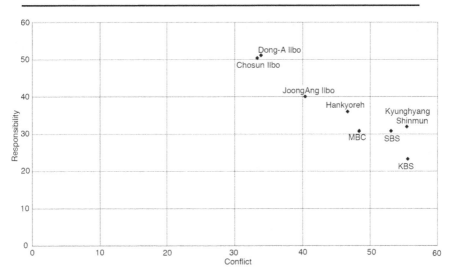

Figure 6–12: Comparison of Media Companies: North Korea's Test Launch of Missiles in 2006 (Conflict vs. Responsibility)

to contribute to peace and stability in the Korean Peninsula and to please its army, which had longed for a powerful self-reliant defense capability. It further claimed that it had become the eighth country to join the club of nuclear weapons states.[25] For North Korea, the possession of a nuclear bomb might serve as symbolizing prestige for its military-first politics, the major device for maintaining power for the Kim dynasty.[26] Although the United States was very cautious in confirming the occurrence of the test, the test appeared to have physically occurred, as the United States Geological Survey publicized that it had detected a tremor of 4.2 magnitude on the Korean Peninsula and South Korea's state-run Earthquake Research Center announced a tremor of 3.58 magnitude in Northern Hamkyong Province, where American satellites had observed suspected underground activities for several years.[27]

North Korea conducted the test two days after the United Nations Security Council warned that a test could lead to "severe consequences." While announcing that the test had ushered in a new era of confrontation with North Korea, the George W. Bush administration called for China and Russia to cut off trade and oil supplies to deter North Korea's proliferation of weapons of mass destruction. U.S. ambassador John Bolton also termed the test "one of the gravest threats to international peace and security."[28]

Although China right after the test registered its firm opposition by defining the test as a "flagrant and brazen violation" of peace in the international community, the Chinese ambassador to the United Nations, Wang Guangya, later recommended 15 member states of the UNSC not to take "provocative steps" to provoke North Korea and called for adopting a "prudent and responsible attitude."[29] North Korea retorted that "threats, sanctions and pressure" from the United States had forced it to declare its possession of nuclear weapons in order to protect its sovereignty and national survival.[30]

The test was also an embarrassment for South Korea's Roh Moo Hyun government, which had adhered to settlements through the six-party talks. It encountered growing domestic criticism and doubts about the effectiveness of the talks. Conservatives raised the issue that financial aid to North Korea might have been used to develop nuclear weapons instead of providing food and other materials to improve living standards.

For this case, a total of 1,169 stories were collected which were published during the one-week period between October 9 and October 15.

TABLE 6–7: MEDIA COVERAGE
OF NORTH KOREA'S NUCLEAR TEST IN 2006

| Media | Number of stories |
|---|---|
| *Chosun Ilbo* | 171 |
| *Joongang Ilbo* | 163 |
| *Donga Ilbo* | 152 |
| *Hankyoreh Shinmun* | 146 |
| *Kyunghyang Shinmun* | 111 |
| KBS | 92 |
| MBC | 66 |
| SBS | 268 |
| TOTAL | 1,169 |

TABLE 6–8: NUMBER OF CASES:
NORTH KOREA'S NUCLEAR TEST IN 2006

| | Chosun Ilbo | Joon-gang Ilbo | Dong-a Ilbo | Hanky-oreh | Kyungh-yang Shinmun | KBS | MBC | SBS | Total |
|---|---|---|---|---|---|---|---|---|---|
| Conflict Frame | 181 | 205 | 175 | 182 | 156 | 129 | 88 | 332 | 1,448 |
| Responsibility Frame | 195 | 176 | 148 | 128 | 89 | 94 | 51 | 278 | 1,159 |
| Crisis Escalation Frame | 59 | 57 | 78 | 95 | 43 | 42 | 39 | 114 | 527 |
| Economic Effect Frame | 78 | 51 | 55 | 33 | 45 | 11 | 20 | 80 | 373 |
| TOTAL | 513 | 489 | 456 | 438 | 333 | 276 | 198 | 804 | 3,507 |

TABLE 6–9: PERCENTAGE OF FRAMES:
NORTH KOREA'S NUCLEAR TEST IN 2006

| | Chosun Ilbo | Joon-gang Ilbo | Dong-a Ilbo | Hanky-oreh | Kyungh-yang Shinmun | KBS | MBC | SBS | Aver-age |
|---|---|---|---|---|---|---|---|---|---|
| Conflict Frame | 35.3 | 41.9 | 38.4 | 41.6 | 46.8 | 46.7 | 44.4 | 41.3 | 41.3 |
| Responsibility Frame | 38.0 | 36.0 | 32.5 | 29.2 | 26.7 | 34.1 | 25.8 | 34.6 | 33.0 |
| Crisis Escalation Frame | 11.5 | 11.7 | 17.1 | 21.7 | 12.9 | 15.2 | 19.7 | 14.2 | 15.0 |

# Social Media and South Korean National Security

| | Chosun Ilbo | Joon-gang Ilbo | Dong-a Ilbo | Hanky-oreh | Kyungh-yang Shinmun | KBS | MBC | SBS | Aver-age |
|---|---|---|---|---|---|---|---|---|---|
| **Economic Effect Frame** | 15.2 | 10.4 | 12.1 | 7.5 | 13.5 | 4.0 | 10.1 | 10.0 | 10.6 |
| TOTAL | 100.0 | 100.0 | 100.0 | 100.0 | 100.0 | 100.0 | 100.0 | 100.0 | 100.0 |

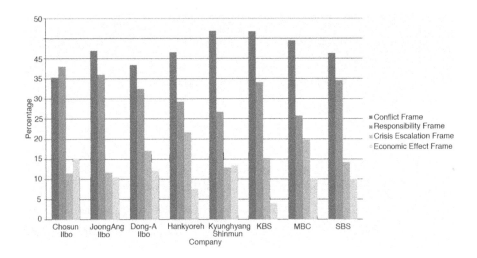

**Figure 6–13: North Korea's Nuclear Test in 2006**

The first nuclear test by North Korea was a shock to the South Korean public. While conservative newspapers criticized North Korea by describing the negative influence of the nuclear test on regional stability and by pointing out Kim Jong-il's provocative character and irresponsibility, liberal newspapers and TV news focused instead on the miscalculated estimation of North Korea's nuclear capability by the South Korean government. Although conservative newspapers demonstrated a balanced use of conflict frames and responsibility frames, all media outlets expressed concern for the changing inter–Korean relations. More specifically, the use of the conflict frame by liberal newspapers and TV news reflected public concern for changes in the inter–Korean military balance brought on by North Korea's nuclear weapon.

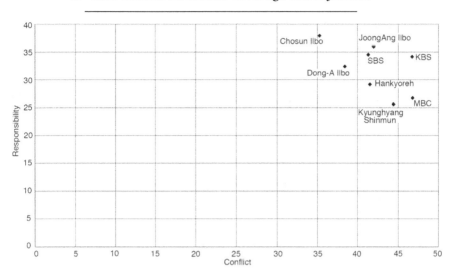

Figure 6–14: Comparison of Media Companies: North Korea's Nuclear Test in 2006 (Conflict vs. Responsibility)

## North Korea's Second Nuclear Test in 2009

North Korea conducted its second nuclear test on May 25, 2009, when it declared that it had successfully conducted another nuclear test "on a new higher level in terms of explosive power and technology" to "bolster its nuclear deterrent for self-defense." The occurrence of the test was confirmed by South Korea's meteorological institution, which detected a tremor of 4.5 in magnitude.[31] The test was the second blow to Washington's pressure on the DPRK to abandon its nuclear program. The test was conducted roughly two months after North Korea launched a long-range missile into the Pacific Ocean on the day U.S. president Barack Obama called for eliminating all nuclear weapons in the world in his speech in Prague.[32]

In a way to tighten sanctions on North Korea, the UNSC passed Resolution 1874 on a unanimous vote of 15 to zero. The resolution was designed to impose an embargo on the shipment of arms from North Korea and a ban on the import of weapons. The resolution reaffirmed that the proliferation of nuclear weapons and other weapons of mass destruction as well as their means of delivery constituted a threat to international peace and security.[33]

### TABLE 6–10: MEDIA COVERAGE OF NORTH KOREA'S NUCLEAR TEST IN 2009

| Media | Number of stories |
|---|---|
| Chosun Ilbo | 116 |
| Joongang Ilbo | 103 |
| Donga Ilbo | 130 |
| Hankyoreh Shinmun | 104 |
| Kyunghyang Shinmun | 94 |
| KBS | 405 |
| MBC | 235 |
| SBS | 144 |
| TOTAL | 1,331 |

### TABLE 6–11: MEDIA COVERAGE OF NORTH KOREA'S NUCLEAR TEST IN 2009

|  | Chosun Ilbo | Joongang Ilbo | Dong-a Ilbo | Hanky-oreh | Kyungh-yang Shinmun | KBS | MBC | SBS | Total |
|---|---|---|---|---|---|---|---|---|---|
| Conflict Frame | 95 | 73 | 132 | 107 | 95 | 468 | 221 | 105 | 1,296 |
| Responsibility Frame | 147 | 134 | 145 | 129 | 126 | 519 | 327 | 205 | 1,732 |
| Crisis Escalation Frame | 78 | 74 | 97 | 44 | 45 | 178 | 113 | 74 | 703 |
| Economic Effect Frame | 28 | 28 | 16 | 32 | 16 | 50 | 44 | 27 | 241 |
| TOTAL | 348 | 309 | 390 | 312 | 282 | 1,215 | 705 | 411 | 3,972 |

### TABLE 6–12: PERCENTAGE OF FRAMES: NORTH KOREA'S NUCLEAR TEST IN 2009

|  | Chosun Ilbo | Joongang Ilbo | Dong-a Ilbo | Hanky-oreh | Kyungh-yang Shinmun | KBS | MBC | SBS | Aver-age |
|---|---|---|---|---|---|---|---|---|---|
| Conflict Frame | 27.3 | 23.6 | 33.8 | 34.3 | 33.7 | 38.5 | 31.3 | 25.5 | 32.6 |
| Responsibility Frame | 42.2 | 43.4 | 37.2 | 41.3 | 44.7 | 42.7 | 46.4 | 49.9 | 43.6 |
| Crisis Escalation Frame | 22.4 | 23.9 | 24.9 | 14.1 | 16.0 | 14.7 | 16.0 | 18.0 | 17.7 |

| | Chosun Ilbo | Joon-gang Ilbo | Dong-a Ilbo | Hanky-oreh | Kyungh-yang Shinmun | KBS | MBC | SBS | Aver-age |
|---|---|---|---|---|---|---|---|---|---|
| Economic Effect Frame | 8.0 | 9.1 | 4.1 | 10.3 | 5.7 | 4.1 | 6.2 | 6.6 | 6.1 |
| TOTAL | 100.0 | 100.0 | 100.0 | 100.0 | 100.0 | 100.0 | 100.0 | 100.0 | 100.0 |

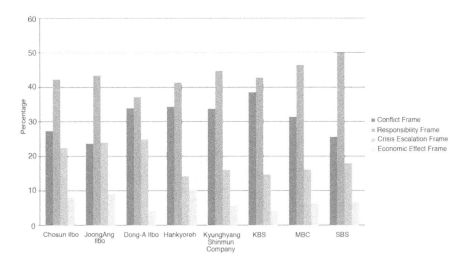

Figure 6–15: North Korea's Second Nuclear Test, 2009

In this case, both conservative and liberal media outlets most frequently demonstrated the usage of the responsibility frame. While the first nuclear test generated concern on possible changes in the inter–Korean military balance because of North Korea's nuclear capability, media response to the second nuclear test was centered on responsibility frames, either blaming the South Korean government for negligent handling of North Korea's nuclear issue or criticizing the war-prone attitude of North Korea.

## The Launch of Long-Range Missile in 2012

After conducting successful nuclear tests, North Korea declared itself a nuclear power and boasted of its nuclear capability

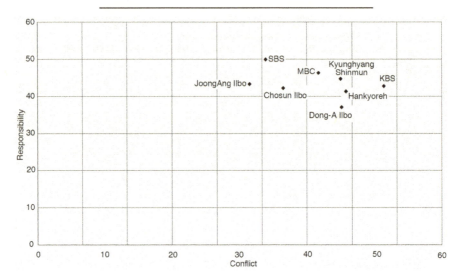

Figure 6–16: Comparison of Media Companies: North Korea's Second Nuclear Test, 2009 (Conflict vs. Responsibility)

to attack the United States. To completely manufacture a nuclear weapon after two successful nuclear tests, North Korea required a missile system that could carry a nuclear warhead weighing around 200 to 300 kilograms. North Korea's launch of long-range missiles was designed to bring the DPRK one step closer to possessing a nuclear weapon that could attack the American mainland. The missile reportedly exploded several minutes after the launch, which implied the test launch was a failure.

A total of 381 stories were collected which were published between April 13 and April 17.

### TABLE 6–13: MEDIA COVERAGE OF NORTH KOREA'S LAUNCH OF LONG-RANGE MISSILE IN 2012

| Media | Number of stories |
|---|---|
| *Chosun Ilbo* | 20 |
| *Joongang Ilbo* | 32 |
| *Donga Ilbo* | 35 |
| *Hankyoreh Shinmun* | 29 |
| *Kyunghyang Shinmun* | 27 |
| KBS | 62 |

142

| Media | Number of stories |
|-------|-------------------|
| MBC | 51 |
| SBS | 125 |
| TOTAL | 381 |

### TABLE 6–14: MEDIA COVERAGE OF NORTH KOREA'S LAUNCH OF LONG-RANGE MISSILE IN 2012

| | Chosun Ilbo | Joon-gang Ilbo | Dong-a Ilbo | Hanky-oreh | Kyungh-yang Shinmun | KBS | MBC | SBS | Total |
|---|---|---|---|---|---|---|---|---|---|
| Conflict Frame | 25 | 43 | 46 | 45 | 34 | 81 | 64 | 142 | 480 |
| Responsibility Frame | 23 | 27 | 37 | 32 | 33 | 76 | 52 | 160 | 440 |
| Crisis Escalation Frame | 12 | 22 | 17 | 10 | 12 | 25 | 31 | 55 | 184 |
| Economic Effect Frame | 0 | 4 | 5 | 0 | 2 | 4 | 6 | 18 | 39 |
| TOTAL | 60 | 96 | 105 | 87 | 81 | 186 | 153 | 375 | 1,143 |

### TABLE 6–15: PERCENTAGE OF FRAMES: NORTH KOREA'S LAUNCH OF LONG-RANGE MISSILE IN 2012

| | Chosun Ilbo | Joon-gang Ilbo | Dong-a Ilbo | Hanky-oreh | Kyungh-yang Shinmun | KBS | MBC | SBS | Aver-age |
|---|---|---|---|---|---|---|---|---|---|
| Conflict Frame | 41.7 | 44.8 | 43.8 | 51.7 | 42.0 | 43.5 | 41.8 | 37.9 | 42.0 |
| Responsibility Frame | 38.3 | 28.1 | 35.2 | 36.8 | 40.7 | 40.9 | 34.0 | 42.7 | 38.5 |
| Crisis Escalation Frame | 20.0 | 22.9 | 16.2 | 11.5 | 14.8 | 13.4 | 20.3 | 14.7 | 16.1 |
| Economic Effect Frame | 0.0 | 4.2 | 4.8 | 0.0 | 2.5 | 2.2 | 3.9 | 4.8 | 3.4 |
| TOTAL | 100.0 | 100.0 | 100.0 | 100.0 | 100.0 | 100.0 | 100.0 | 100.0 | 100.0 |

As shown in the figures, most media except SBS used the conflict frame more frequently than the responsibility frame, which implies serious concern for the increased capability of North Korea's nuclear weapons program. North Korea's shelling of Yeonpyeong Island showed that the threat of North Korean aggression was real and that a nuclear attack on the South might not be ruled out as an option for North Korea.

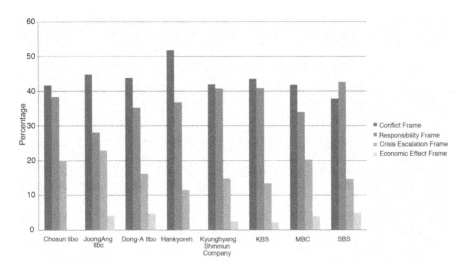

Figure 6–17: North Korea's Launch of Long-range Missile in 2012

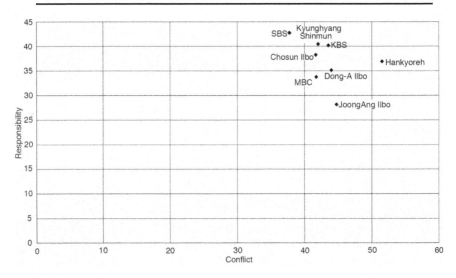

Figure 6–18: Comparison of Media Companies: North Korea's Launch of Long-range Missile in 2012 (Conflict vs. Responsibility)

With regard to social media coverage between April 13 and April 17, 2012, a total of 4,548 users tweeted 7,610 messages; 3,758 users tweeted 6,796 messages with the key words, "North Korean missile"; and 790 users tweeted 814 opinions with the key words

"North Korean long-range missile." On the day of the launch, 3,628 messages were tweeted. The number decreased sharply on the following day, April 14, with 1,101 messages.

TABLE 6–16: NUMBER OF MENTIONS:
LAUNCH OF LONG-RANGE MISSILE

| Dates | Keywords: North Korean long-range missile | Keywords: North Korean missile | Sum |
|---|---|---|---|
| April 13, 2012 | 727 | 2,901 | 3,628 |
| April 14 | 55 | 1,046 | 1,101 |
| April 15 | 11 | 817 | 828 |
| April 16 | 19 | 923 | 942 |
| April 17 | 2 | 1,109 | 1,111 |

Following the test launch of the long-range missile, most messages focused on the incompetency of the South Korean government in managing North Korea's continued provocations and at the same time ridiculed the despotic rule of Kim Jong-un and his failure in the missile test. The most frequently retweeted message (687 retweets) called for a united and nonpartisan voice against North Korea's weapons of mass destruction by sarcastically portraying South Korea's liberal politicians as "dumb" to North Korea's repeated provocations of nuclear and missile tests. The message criticized the silence about the test launch from politicians who were only concerned with political struggles against each other and had little interest in security affairs. The message appeared to be very sarcastic about pro–North Korea politicians leading a political party which was silent about North Korea's provocations.

Another message that was retweeted 670 times also carried cynical criticism regarding Kim Jong-un. It said that he might execute missile technicians for the failure of the test launch, much as he had executed his deputy defense minister, who drank alcoholic beverages during the mourning period for Kim Jong-il. One message that was retweeted 172 times concerned the negligence of the South Korean government in dealing with North Korea's missile launch by indicating North Korea's missiles could have targeted South

Korea. It also made mention of the fact that Japan had deployed Patriot missiles in a park full of cherry blossoms to defend against North Korea's missiles. Another message that was retweeted 171 times criticized the pro–North Korean stance of the Unified Progressive Party by quoting its blaming of the United States and the United Nations instead of North Korea. Another message also worried about North Korea's capability to complete its development of a long-range missile in the near future despite its current failure. This message was retweeted 102 times. Another message that criticized the party's silence was retweeted 70 times. There was also a tweet that mentioned opposition leaders' names when it criticized the opposition party's silence on North Korea's provocation.

## The Launch of the Unha-3 Long-Range Missile in 2012

At 9:51 a.m. on December 12, 2012, North Korea launched a long-range rocket which was detected in orbit by the North American Aerospace Defense Command. North Korea hailed the launch as a success by mentioning that "(t)he second version of the satellite Kwangmyongsong-3 successfully lifted off from the Sohae Space Center on the carrier rocket Unha-3." South Korea and the United States termed the launch a highly provocative act. United Nations secretary general Ban Ki-moon also criticized the launch as a "clear violation of UNSC Resolutions 1718 and 1874," which banned any launch of ballistic missiles. The launch signified the improved capability of North Korea in its pursuit of nuclear weapons. Some 846 stories between December 12, 2012, and January 23, 2013, were collected.

TABLE 6–17: MEDIA COVERAGE OF NORTH KOREA'S
LAUNCH OF UNHA-3 IN 2012

| Media | Number of stories |
|---|---|
| *Chosun Ilbo* | 115 |
| *Joongang Ilbo* | 108 |
| *Donga Ilbo* | 103 |

| Media | Number of stories |
|---|---|
| *Hankyoreh Shinmun* | 18 |
| *Kyunghyang Shinmun* | 85 |
| KBS | 114 |
| MBC | 134 |
| SBS | 169 |
| TOTAL | 846 |

TABLE 6–18: MEDIA COVERAGE OF NORTH KOREA'S
LAUNCH OF UNHA-3 IN 2012

| | Chosun Ilbo | Joon-gang Ilbo | Dong-a Ilbo | Hanky-oreh | Kyungh-yang Shinmun | KBS | MBC | SBS | Total |
|---|---|---|---|---|---|---|---|---|---|
| Conflict Frame | 140 | 113 | 100 | 26 | 105 | 140 | 131 | 170 | 925 |
| Responsibility Frame | 135 | 127 | 118 | 18 | 87 | 124 | 173 | 225 | 1,007 |
| Crisis Escalation Frame | 64 | 81 | 84 | 10 | 60 | 63 | 92 | 87 | 541 |
| Economic Effect Frame | 6 | 3 | 7 | 0 | 3 | 15 | 0 | 25 | 59 |
| TOTAL | 345 | 324 | 309 | 54 | 255 | 342 | 396 | 507 | 2,532 |

TABLE 6–19: PERCENTAGE OF FRAMES:
NORTH KOREA'S LAUNCH OF UNHA-3 IN 2012

| | Chosun Ilbo | Joon-gang Ilbo | Dong-a Ilbo | Hanky-oreh | Kyungh-yang Shinmun | KBS | MBC | SBS | Aver-age |
|---|---|---|---|---|---|---|---|---|---|
| Conflict Frame | 40.6 | 34.9 | 32.4 | 48.1 | 41.2 | 40.9 | 33.1 | 33.5 | 36.5 |
| Responsibility Frame | 39.1 | 39.2 | 38.2 | 33.3 | 34.1 | 36.3 | 43.7 | 44.4 | 39.8 |
| Crisis Escalation Frame | 18.6 | 25.0 | 27.2 | 18.5 | 23.5 | 18.4 | 23.2 | 17.2 | 21.4 |
| Economic Effect Frame | 1.7 | 0.9 | 2.3 | 0.0 | 1.2 | 4.4 | 0.0 | 4.9 | 2.3 |
| TOTAL | 100.0 | 100.0 | 100.0 | 100.0 | 100.0 | 100.0 | 100.0 | 100.0 | 100.0 |

As with the failed test in April, most media outlets employed conflict frames expressing concern over the increasing capability of North Korea's nuclear arsenal and the widening military imbalance with North Korea.

On the successful launch of the North Korea's Unha-3 missile,

147

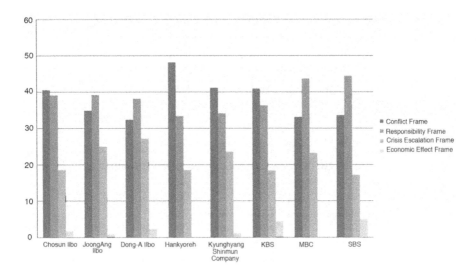

**Figure 6–19: North Korea's Launch of Unha-3 in 2012**

6,430 tweeters uploaded 8,815 messages. Among them, 4,036 messages were tweeted on the day of the launch, implying SNS influence was short-term and limited. The number of tweets decreased to 1,643 on the following day.

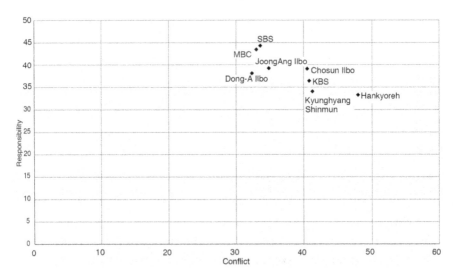

**Figure 6–20: Comparison of Media Companies: North Korea's Launch of Unha-3 in 2012 (Conflict vs. Responsibility)**

TABLE 6–20: NUMBER OF MENTIONS:
LAUNCH OF UNHA-3 MISSILE

| 1st 5 days: 7,184 | | | | | 2nd 5 days: 432 | | | | | | 3rd 5 days: 126 | | | |
|---|---|---|---|---|---|---|---|---|---|---|---|---|---|---|
| 12 | 13 | 14 | 15 | 16 | 17 | 18 | 19 | 20 | 21 | 22 | 23 | 24 | 25 | 26 |
| 4036 | 1643 | 773 | 378 | 354 | 236 | 104 | 66 | 21 | 5 | 16 | 39 | 22 | 11 | 38 |

The number of messages showed a sharp decrease from 7,184 in the first week to 126 in the third week. One may find two reasons for the sharp decrease. First, public attention was transferred from North Korea's launch of long-range missile to South Korea's presidential election on December 19. Most retweeted messages were also related to the presidential election, mostly evaluating the influence of North Korea's missile launch on each presidential candidate. In particular, some messages indicated that the launch could be detrimental to the liberal candidate because it would increase cohesion among conservative voters. Another message cited the irresponsibility of the opposition party for its criticisms against the government by indicating North Korea's nuclear and missile provocations took place during the Kim Dae-jung and Roh Moo Hyun governments.

Other messages evaluated the launch as having a negative impact on the ruling party, focusing on its incompetence in deterring North Korea's provocative behaviors. A message that was retweeted 335 times assessed that the launch would exert a positive influence on the opposition candidate, Moon Jae-in, while another message retweeted 257 times also portrayed the launch as covering fire for supporting Moon. Other messages were overall negative toward the government. A message retweeted 202 times criticized the government for doing nothing but releasing scenes of emergency meetings held in the Blue House bunker, while also noting the email distribution by the Japanese government to the local authorities regarding North Korea's missile launch. One message not favorable to the opposition party, retweeted 176 times, criticized Moon's deliberate comparison of the success of the Unha-3 missile with South Korea's failure in launching the Naro satellite. Another

149

message retweeted 103 times blamed pro–North Korean groups by raising a question whether they would claim the return of Unha-3 parts collected by the South Korean navy.

## *North Korea's Provocations*

### The Sinking of ROKS *Cheonan* in 2010

The sinking of ROKS *Cheonan* was the first case in which official governmental announcements were challenged by media discourse formulated by internet news and social media. At 9:22 p.m. on March 26, 2010, South Korea's 1,200-ton Navy vessel ROKS *Cheonan* was sunk by a North Korean torpedo attack in the West Sea, where repeated naval clashes had taken place between the two Koreas. The sinking killed 46 crew members out of 104, all of whom were conducting a normal patrol mission in the vicinity of Baengnyeong Island. The sinking shocked and angered most South Koreans. More than a few were skeptical about North Korea's involvement in the attack.

As the South Korean government publicly announced that it was a North Korean torpedo fired by one of its midget submarines which sank the ship, North Korea firmly denied the accusation. In addition, it successfully avoided being identified as the attacker with support from China and Russia when the UNSC issued a presidential statement condemning the attack without identifying the attacker.

The media covered deep skepticisms registered by opposition politicians. For example, an opposition member of the National Assembly, Choi Moon-soon, messaged during his interview with *Time* on August 13 that the ship probably ran aground without a North Korean attack and that the government's accusation was a fabrication aiming at influencing the local election scheduled on June 2. He also raised strong doubts that the Lee Myung-bak government would ever publish any report whatsoever with regard to the sinking.[34]

When the South Korean government officially announced that

the ship was split and sunk due to "shockwave and bubble effect generated by underwater explosion" of a torpedo fired by a North Korean submarine, it also presented shattered parts of the sunken vessel and the remains of a torpedo for evidence. The government-led investigation team, including 24 foreign experts from the United States, the United Kingdom, Sweden and Australia, announced that the weapon system that sank ROKS *Cheonan* was a CHT-02D torpedo manufactured by North Korea.[35]

The official announcement was then challenged by opposition leaders and citizen activists who argued the ship was sunk due to other causes, such as accidental collision with a reef. The media conveyed growing skepticisms voiced by opposition leaders, liberal citizens, and antigovernment and pro–North Korean activists. The investigation team dismissed any possibility of a non-explosion by indicating that the sonar system remained intact on the ship's bottom, which could be a countervailing proof against the accidental collision scenario raised by citizen activists. The team also explained that the crooked propeller on the right was bent not because of collision with a reef but due to "inertial force" generated by the abrupt halt of operations, thereby refuting the collision scenario. However, the team failed to prove the ink used in the marking "no. 1" written on one of the torpedo remains was manufactured in North Korea.

For this case, 6,304 stories were collected which were published and aired between March 26 and July 1.

TABLE 6–21: MEDIA COVERAGE
OF THE SINKING OF ROKS CHEONAN

| Media | Number of stories |
|---|---|
| *Chosun Ilbo* | 675 |
| *Joongang Ilbo* | 785 |
| *Donga Ilbo* | 651 |
| *Hankyoreh Shinmun* | 587 |
| *Kyunghyang Shinmun* | 680 |
| KBS | 1,490 |
| MBC | 912 |
| SBS | 524 |
| TOTAL | 6,304 |

### TABLE 6–22: MEDIA COVERAGE
### OF THE SINKING OF ROKS CHEONAN

|  | Chosun Ilbo | Joon-gang Ilbo | Dong-a Ilbo | Hanky-oreh | Kyungh-yang Shinmun | KBS | MBC | SBS | Total |
|---|---|---|---|---|---|---|---|---|---|
| Conflict Frame | 394 | 505 | 423 | 363 | 428 | 1,159 | 556 | 353 | 4,181 |
| Responsibility Frame | 789 | 1,159 | 834 | 936 | 990 | 1,988 | 1,257 | 662 | 8,615 |
| Crisis Escalation Frame | 157 | 140 | 96 | 118 | 152 | 280 | 101 | 54 | 1,098 |
| Economic Effect Frame | 43 | 70 | 85 | 64 | 71 | 91 | 62 | 16 | 502 |
| Human Interest Frame | 642 | 481 | 515 | 280 | 399 | 952 | 760 | 487 | 4,516 |
| TOTAL | 2,025 | 2,355 | 1,953 | 1,761 | 2,040 | 4,470 | 2,736 | 1,572 | 18,912 |

### TABLE 6–23: PERCENTAGE OF FRAMES:
### SINKING OF ROKS CHEONAN

|  | Chosun Ilbo | Joon-gang Ilbo | Dong-a Ilbo | Hanky-oreh | Kyungh-yang Shinmun | KBS | MBC | SBS | Aver-age |
|---|---|---|---|---|---|---|---|---|---|
| Conflict Frame | 19.5 | 21.4 | 21.7 | 20.6 | 21.0 | 25.9 | 20.3 | 22.5 | 22.1 |
| Responsibility Frame | 39.0 | 49.2 | 42.7 | 53.2 | 48.5 | 44.5 | 45.9 | 42.1 | 45.6 |
| Crisis Escalation Frame | 7.8 | 5.9 | 4.9 | 6.7 | 7.5 | 6.3 | 3.7 | 3.4 | 5.8 |
| Economic Effect Frame | 2.1 | 3.0 | 4.4 | 3.6 | 3.5 | 2.0 | 2.3 | 1.0 | 2.7 |
| Human Interest Frame | 31.7 | 20.4 | 26.4 | 15.9 | 19.6 | 21.3 | 27.8 | 31.0 | 23.9 |
| TOTAL | 100.0 | 100.0 | 100.0 | 100.0 | 100.0 | 100.0 | 100.0 | 100.0 | 100.0 |

Most media coverage of the sinking of ROKS *Cheonan* employed the responsibility frame, in which conservative and liberal media debated over who was responsible for the sinking. In addition, the human interest frame was also employed to convey stories of victims and their family members.

When ROKS *Cheonan* was sunk on March 26, 2010, the South Korean government registered an official announcement that the 1,200-ton patrol ship was sunk by a torpedo attack by North Korea.

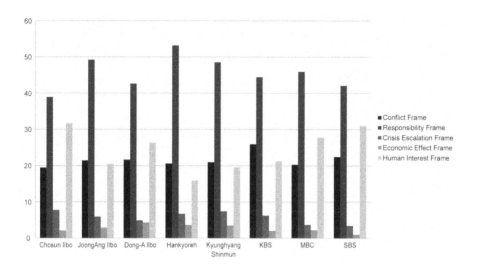

**Figure 6–21:  The Sinking of ROKS *Cheonan***

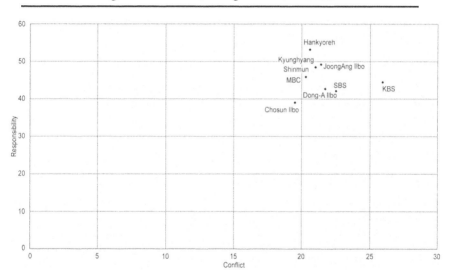

**Figure 6–22:  Comparison of Media Companies: The Sinking of ROKS *Cheonan* (Conflict vs. Responsibility)**

The official announcement was challenged by unconfirmed rumors on social media that the ROKS *Cheonan* was sunk by a friendly torpedo fired from a U.S. vessel that was participating in a joint military exercise or was sunk by friction with the bottom of the shallow sea.

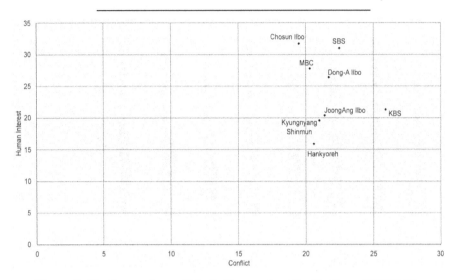

**Figure 6–23: Comparison of Media Companies: The Sinking of ROKS *Cheonan* (Conflict vs. Human Interest)**

Some rumors suggested that the South Korean government intentionally concealed the real cause of the sinking in order to prompt an inter–Korean summit.

Repeated requests by the media in the midst of increased public distrust and rumors spread by social media drove the ministry to release an 80-second-long thermal observation video excerpt from a 40-minute-long video. Then Defense Minister Kim Tae-young presented a brief about thermal observation results that showed the ROKS *Cheonan* was broken into two parts on March 27, 2010, thereby reversing the ministry's refusal to release the content of thermal observation to the media. All records of communication were classified and remained out of access by the media. *Kyunghyang Shinmun* suggested the military's excessive control of information increased distrust regarding the government's announcement about the sinking of ROKS *Cheonan*.[36]

Faced with calls for complete public disclosure of the split hull of the ROKS *Cheonan*, the military rejected the calls because fulfilling them would make public the classified inner structure of

South Korean military vessels. In particular, the ministry further explained that the width of outer steel sheets and intra-sheet structures were highly sensitive military secrets. The ministry further said that young navy sailors were still on board more than 20 patrol ships with similar inner structures.[37]

Kim Hak-song, chairman of the defense committee of the South Korean National Assembly, released the content of a classified briefing by the Ministry of Defense that the South Korean military had failed to trace one of two North Korean submarines operating in the West Sea on the day of the sinking of ROKS *Cheonan*, while the other had been detected to be in communication with its base. This classified information disclosed weak points of the ROK's submarine detection posture. Conservative media like *Chosun Ilbo* warned those politician leakers about making sensitive military information public, while liberal media like *Kyunghyang Shinmun* complained about excessive secrecy, since the South Korean military refused to release the contents of communication records between ROKS *Cheonan* and the naval base.[38]

Again, the release of sensitive military secrets by the media took place in November of the same year. One opposition member of the National Assembly mentioned that North Korea did not have to send spies to South Korea due to the excessive release of military information in the media.[39] After the shelling of Yeonpyeong Island by North Korean artillery on November 23, 2010, detailed reports by the South Korean media about the scale, range and overall capacity of weapons deployed on that island revealed sensitive military information that could be used by North Korea. The Defense Ministry requested reporters stationed on Yeonpyeong Island to leave the island for their safety, but reporters refused to leave because there were 31 residents on the island and the government could not ban reporting even in combat.[40]

Reports by *Donga Ilbo* about the poor management of artillery on the west coast could have revealed weak points of South Korea's defense condition. However, the editor decided to carry that article to warn the military of rotten management of the artillery.[41] Detailed briefings on military affairs at the assembly hearings disclosed arms deployment at the battlefield. On November 30, 2010, Defense Minister Kim Tae-young's testimony disclosed the plan to deploy Pegasus land-to-air missiles on the island of Yeonpyeong and his confession of miscalculation of the North Korean threat of artillery to the island.[42]

Figure 6–24 demonstrates that the number of daily debates on *Agora* saw a dramatic increase from 79 on May 1 to 1,872 on May 20, when the government officially released its review results of why the ship sank. Before the release of the official report of the governmental analysis of the sinking, 683 was the highest number of daily debates, on March 29, three days after the sinking. The decrease of the number of daily debates was reversed dramatically on May 20, thereby signifying social media's contribution in

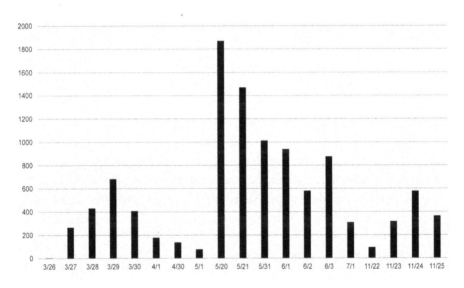

Figure 6–24: Number of Daily Debates on *Agora*
Source: *Tae-Eun Song, "The Multitude's Foreign Policy Debates and its Collective Behavior through Social Media: The Impact of Changing Communication Environment on the Public's Foreign Policy Attitudes,"* Korean Journal of International Relations, *53:1 (2013), p. 61.*

triggering public distrust of the government's official report on the sinking.

## The Shelling of Yeonpyeong Island in 2010

On November 22, 2010, North Korea fired a barrage of about 100 artillery shells onto the island of Yeonpyeong, killing two marines and two civilians and wounding 13 others. The North Korean shells started to fall onto the island which is located about 50 miles away from Incheon at 2:34 p.m. and stopped around at 4:42 p.m. The South Korean military returned fire with about 80 shells towards the North Korean artillery sites, deployed F-16 fighter jets and put all South Korean troops on maximum alert. The South Korean army's joint chief of staff, Han Min-koo, and General Walter Sharp, commander of the 28,500 U.S. troops stationed in South Korea, registered solemn warnings which were followed by President Lee's statement to resolutely deal with the shelling and to make all-out efforts not to aggravate the situation. The White House press secretary also made it clear that the United States was "firmly committed" to the defense of South Korea and also to the "maintenance of regional peace and stability."[43]

The shelling ignited another round of debates about who was responsible. The shells were fired while the South Korean navy was conducting a routine nine-day annual drill near the island. The "Hoguk Exercise," one of three major annual military exercises, against which the North had registered a message of denouncement that termed the drill as provocation, had started and involved about 70,000 troops.[44]

Opposition leaders and pro–North Korean activists criticized the South Korean government for launching the drills in spite of repeated warnings by North Korea. The South Korean government argued it was a regular drill aimed at the southwest, the opposite direction from North Korea.

A total of 3,016 stories were collected, which were published between November 23, 2010, and January 21, 2011.

### TABLE 6–24: MEDIA COVERAGE
### OF THE SHELLING OF YEONPYEONG ISLAND

| Media | Number of stories |
|---|---|
| *Chosun Ilbo* | 424 |
| *Joongang Ilbo* | 304 |
| *Donga Ilbo* | 306 |
| *Hankyoreh Shinmun* | 415 |
| *Kyunghyang Shinmun* | 398 |
| KBS | 606 |
| MBC | 301 |
| SBS | 262 |
| TOTAL | 3,016 |

### TABLE 6–25: MEDIA COVERAGE
### OF THE SHELLING OF YEONPYEONG ISLAND

| | *Chosun Ilbo* | *Joongang Ilbo* | *Dong-a Ilbo* | *Hankyoreh* | *Kyunghyang Shinmun* | KBS | MBC | SBS | Total |
|---|---|---|---|---|---|---|---|---|---|
| Conflict Frame | 343 | 308 | 317 | 474 | 422 | 660 | 346 | 307 | 3,177 |
| Responsibility Frame | 434 | 324 | 352 | 451 | 446 | 589 | 225 | 207 | 3,028 |
| Crisis Escalation Frame | 190 | 113 | 80 | 127 | 143 | 329 | 194 | 142 | 1,318 |
| Economic Effect Frame | 42 | 23 | 61 | 52 | 71 | 105 | 58 | 69 | 481 |
| Human Interest Frame | 263 | 144 | 108 | 141 | 112 | 135 | 80 | 61 | 1,044 |
| TOTAL | 1,272 | 912 | 918 | 1,245 | 1,194 | 1,818 | 903 | 786 | 9,048 |

### TABLE 6–26: PERCENTAGE OF FRAME:
### THE SHELLING OF YEONPYEONG ISLAND

| | *Chosun Ilbo* | *Joongang Ilbo* | *Dong-a Ilbo* | *Hankyoreh* | *Kyunghyang Shinmun* | KBS | MBC | SBS | Average |
|---|---|---|---|---|---|---|---|---|---|
| Conflict Frame | 27.0 | 33.8 | 34.5 | 38.1 | 35.3 | 36.3 | 38.3 | 39.1 | 35.1 |
| Responsibility Frame | 34.1 | 35.5 | 38.3 | 36.2 | 37.4 | 32.4 | 24.9 | 26.3 | 33.5 |
| Crisis Escalation Frame | 14.9 | 12.4 | 8.7 | 10.2 | 12.0 | 18.1 | 21.5 | 18.1 | 14.6 |
| Economic Effect Frame | 3.3 | 2.5 | 6.6 | 4.2 | 5.9 | 5.8 | 6.4 | 8.8 | 5.3 |

| | Chosun Ilbo | Joon-gang Ilbo | Dong-a Ilbo | Hanky-oreh | Kyungh-yang Shinmun | KBS | MBC | SBS | Aver-age |
|---|---|---|---|---|---|---|---|---|---|
| Human Interest Frame | 20.7 | 15.8 | 11.8 | 11.3 | 9.4 | 7.4 | 8.9 | 7.8 | 11.5 |
| TOTAL | 100.0 | 100.0 | 100.0 | 100.0 | 100.0 | 100.0 | 100.0 | 100.0 | 100.0 |

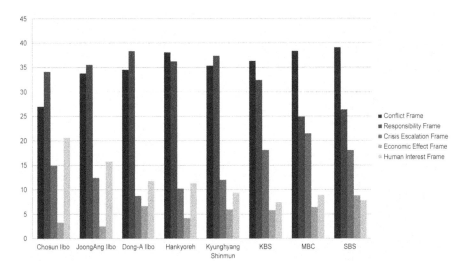

**Figure 6–25: The Shelling of Yeonpyeong Island**

Media coverage of the shelling of Yeonpyeong demonstrated balanced use of the conflict frame and the responsibility frame. The exchange of artillery fire between the two Koreas generated conflict frames, while responsibility frames were used to debate over who or what triggered North Korea's shelling.

Regarding the Yeonpyeong bombardment, 349 users tweeted 6,849 messages between November 23 and January 21. The most frequently tweeted messages were antigovernment rather than anti–North Korean. One statement tweeted 117 times sarcastically criticized the incompetence of the Lee Myungbak government: "the burning of Namdaemoon was covered up by [the news of] Yongsan burning which was then covered up by the sinking of ROKS *Cheonan*. The sinking of ROKS *Cheonan* was covered up by the Yeonpyong shelling which was covered up by foot-mouth disease, which was also covered up by winter coldness. The [Lee] government seems to be rice topped with accidents in which the government tried to cover up previous mistakes by following mistakes[. W]hat will they use to cover up the winter ... coldness?"

An unconfirmed rumor was one of the most tweeted items in the social media. One message tweeted 44 times spread an unconfirmed story about a visit by Kathleen Stephens, then American ambassador to South Korea, and Walter Sharpe, then commander of U.S. troops in South Korea, to the Blue House. It argued the visit was allegedly to ask whether the artillery exercise by the South Korean army conducted one day before the Yeonpyeong bombing was necessary. It was reported that the visit was to express U.S. will to support South Korea. The connotation carried by the message was that North Korea's bombardment of the island was triggered by South Korea's artillery exercise and that the Seoul government was responsible.

Another message (tweeted 20 times) carried complaints about claimed unjust searches declared to be conducted by the government:

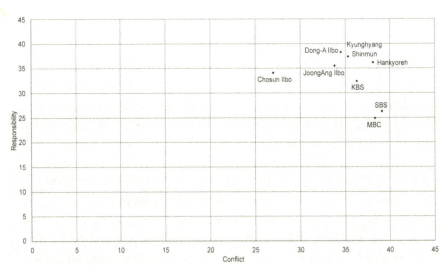

**Figure 6–26: Comparison of Media Companies: The Shelling of Yeonpyeong Island (Conflict vs. Responsibility)**

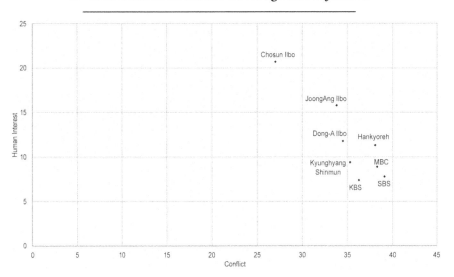

Figure 6–27: Comparison of Media Companies: The Shelling of Yeonpyeong Island (Conflict vs. Human Interest)

"I was subject to [un]warranted search and seizure after I had mentioned the fundamental source of the bombardment was generated from the northern limitation line (NLL)." The message by Mr. Cho was tweeted 18 times to spread his complaints that he had allegedly been indicted for mentioning on Twitter that the bombardment was triggered by South Korea's artillery drill, despite repeated warnings by North Korea. As the last part of his message, he added a question: "what do you think about this?" Another message was tweeted 15 times: "Men killed by the sinking of ROKS *Cheonan* and the bombardment of Yeonpyong, animals killed by foot-and-mouth decease [disease], land ransacked by the Four River Projects, Dokdo omitted in the Defense White Paper, pro–Japanese traitors fattened by a broadcasting project, citizens angered by the nominee for the director of the Board of Audit and Inspection who accepted a hundred thousand dollars in legal service fees."

Another message tweeted 13 times criticized the ruling party for blaming others without taking responsibility. "Responsibility for North Korea's nuclear bomb and the sinking of ROKS *Cheonan* is on the Sunshine policy and the responsibility of spread of foot-and-mouth disease is on the opposition party which led a nationwide campaign. What a comfortable choice." One message indicated the difference in the life cycle of a story on Twitter and on the conventional media. The message, tweeted 14 times, indicated that the news about foot-and-mouth disease could be found only on the web, while conventional media no longer talked about the issue, contrary to their several-months' handling of the sinking of ROKS *Cheonan* and the shelling of Yeonpyeong Island.

## Inter–Korean Relations

Inter–Korean relations during the Lee Myung-bak government became stalemated due to the death of a female tourist at Mount Kumkang, the sinking of ROKS *Cheonan* in March 2010 and the shelling of Yeonpyeong Island later in the same year. The May 24 sanctions imposed a comprehensive package of economic penalties in a way to compel North Korea to admit its sinking of ROKS *Cheonan*, in which North Korea denied being involved. Whether to lift the May 24 sanction has become a hotly debated item in South Korea's domestic politics.

On August 22, 2013, North Korean Red Cross accepted the request by its South Korean counterpart to hold working-level talks over a variety of issues, including the reunion of separated families, the reopening of Mount Kumkang tourism and the resumption of the Kaesong Industrial Complex. A collection of messages, replies, and tweets between August 22 and August 28, 2013, showed the trends of public views over inter–Korean relations appearing on social media.[45]

### The Closure of Kaesong Industrial Complex in 2013

Kaesong Industrial Complex had been a symbol of inter–Korean economic cooperation since its opening in 2005 until its closure in February 2016.

TABLE 6–27: BRIEF HISTORY OF KAESONG INDUSTRIAL
COMPLEX AND CONDITIONS

| Year | Event | N. Korean workers (N) | S. Korean workers (N) | Fabs (N) | Production (million $) | Trade In/Out (million $) |
|------|-------|------------------------|------------------------|----------|------------------------|--------------------------|
| 2000 | **Aug.** Hyundai and Asia-Pacific Peace Committee of N. Korea reached an agreement on launching Kaesong Industrial Complex (Total: 66.1 million square meters) | — | — | — | — | — |
| 2002 | **Nov.** North Korea enacted the Special Laws on Kaesong Industrial Complex | — | — | — | — | — |
| 2003 | **June.** Held 1st phase of ground-breaking ceremony of Kaesong Industrial Complex (3.3 million square meters) | — | — | — | — | — |
| 2004 | **June.** Completion of preparation of pilot industrial site **Dec.** Released first production of Kaesong Industrial Park, kitchen wares | — | — | — | — | 42 |
| 2005 | **Sept.** Moved 24 S. Korean fabs into Kaesong Industrial Complex | 6,013 | 507 | 18 | 781 | 177 |
| 2006 | **May.** Completion of 1st phase of land construction in Kaesong Industrial Park (3.3 million square meters) **Nov.** Marked the employment of 10,000 N. Korean workers | 11,160 | 791 | 30 | | 299 |
| 2007 | **June.** Moved 183 S. Korean fabs into Kaesong Industrial Complex | 22,538 | 785 | 65 | | 441 |
| 2008 | **Dec.** N. Korea limited the number of Kaesong Industrial Complex resident S. Koreans to 880 | 38,931 | 1,055 | 93 | | 808 |
| 2009 | **June.** N. Korea suggested wage claim at one worker per $300 monthly and using rate of Kaesong land at $500 million | 42,561 | 935 | 117 | | 941 |

| Year | Event | N. Korean workers (N) | S. Korean workers (N) | Fabs (N) | Production (million $) | Trade In/Out (million $) |
|---|---|---|---|---|---|---|
| 2010 | **May.** S. Korean government banned new investment in Kaesong Industrial Complex due to *Cheonan* sinking | 46,284 | 804 | 121 | 323 | 1,443 |
|  | **Nov.** S. Korea banned visits to Kaesong Industrial Complex due to Yeonpyeong shelling incident by N. Korea |  |  |  |  |  |
| 2011 | **Jan.** N. Korea announced the working group talks on Kaesong Industrial Complex | 49,866 | 776 | 123 | 402 | 1,698 |
| 2012 | **Jan.** Marked the employment of 50,000 N. Korean workers | 53,448 | 786 | 123 | 470 | 1,961 |
| 2013 | **April–May.** All N. and S. Korean workers evacuated from Kaesong Industrial Complex, and Kaesong Industrial Complex temporally shut down **June.** German company Groz-Beckert set up the fab in Kaesong Industrial Complex **Sept.** Reoperation of Kaesong Industrial Complex | 52,329 | 757 | 123 | 224 | 1,132 |
| 2014 | **Dec.** N. Korea revised the wage regulation | 53,947 | 815 | 125 | 470 | 2,338 |
| 2015 | **Aug.** Both Koreas reached an agreement on raising the minimum wage of N. Korean workers at 5 percent | 54,763 | 803 | 124 | 563 | 2,704 |
| 2016 | **Feb.** S. Korean government limited S. Korean access to Kaesong Industrial Complex due to N. Korea's missile launching and announced the decision to shut down Kaesong Industrial Complex completely | — | — | — | — | — |

*Source: Home pages of Ministry of Unification, Kaesong Industrial Complex and Hyundai Asan Corporation, which are open to public at https://www.kidmac.com/kor/contents.do?menuNo=100158; https:nkinfo.unikorea.go.kr; http://www.gaesong.net/korean/portal.php; http://www.hyundai-asan.com/*

In 2013, North Korea unilaterally suspended the operation of the complex due to the U.S.–South Korean joint military exercise in April. The suspension lasted for almost five months before both sides agreed to reopen the complex. The following table was the result of analysis of tweets with the keywords "Kaesong Industrial Complex" between August 22 and 28, 2013.

**TABLE 6–28: SOCIAL MEDIA
ON KAESONG INDUSTRIAL COMPLEX IN 2013**

| | Date | Mentions | Replies | Tweets | Total |
|---|---|---|---|---|---|
| Kaesong Industrial Complex | Aug. 23, 2013 | 390 | 5 | 83 | 478 |
| | Aug. 27, 2013 | 1,154 | 47 | 736 | 1,937 |
| | Aug. 28, 2013 | 128 | 4 | 71 | 203 |
| | SUBTOTAL | 4,704 | 201 | 2,126 | 7,031 |

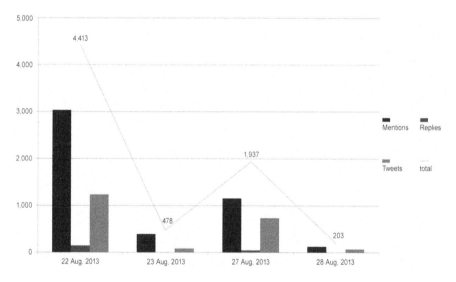

Figure 6–28: Social Media on Kaesong Industrial Complex in 2013

The most frequent messages were "6 million dollars" and "money transfer to the North." Social media mentions portrayed the Park government's humanitarian aid of $6 million through UNICEF as merely a money transfer to North Korea without specifying that it was humanitarian aid through UNICEF. In addition, social media reported conservative politicians' criticisms that the Kim Dae-jung government's financial aid to the North contributed to the progress of North Korea's nuclear bomb development. It added that conservatives had no right to accuse the Kim government's financial aid to the North because the Park government had done the same. Some criticized conservative claims that the Park government succeeded in generating North Korea's consent to reopen the complex without paying financial compensation.

TABLE 6–29: MOST FREQUENTLY MENTIONED WORDS:
KAESONG INDUSTRIAL COMPLEX, 2013

| Rank | Aug. 22, 2013 | | Aug. 23, 2013 | | Aug. 27, 2013 | | Aug. 28, 2013 | |
|---|---|---|---|---|---|---|---|---|
| | word | N | word | N | word | N | word | N |
| 1 | RT | 2,861 | RT | 355 | RT | 1,313 | Kaesong Industrial Complex | 160 |
| 2 | Kaesong Industrial Complex | 2,613 | Luckyline7 | 196 | Kaesong Industrial Complex | 1,090 | RT | 138 |
| 3 | $6 million | 699 | Park Geun-hye | 194 | Luckyline7 | 528 | Common Committee | 70 |
| 4 | To North Korea | 688 | North Korean side | 190 | Park Geun-hye | 489 | South & North | 55 |
| 5 | Park Geun-hye | 653 | approval | 190 | without | 442 | maisana 2002 | 51 |
| 6 | 4 | 533 | $6 million | 190 | what? | 437 | organization | 51 |
| 7 | after | 465 | Sending money to North Korea | 190 | $6 million | 428 | Agreement | 49 |
| 8 | give | 448 | Kaesong Industrial Complex | 179 | Sending money to North Korea | 428 | Breaking news | 48 |
| 9 | For Kaesong Industrial Complex | 445 | Park Geun-hye would | 143 | North Korean side | 426 | Thing | 47 |
| 10 | Kim Dae-Jung | 436 | Byun Hee-jae | 143 | approval | 416 | There is | 45 |

### TABLE 6–30: TWEETS ON KAESONG INDUSTRIAL COMPLEX

| Date | ID | In-Degree | Out-Degree | Betweenness Centrality | Closeness Centrality | Eigenvector Centrality | Tweets |
|---|---|---|---|---|---|---|---|
| Aug. 22, 2013 | V***** | 243 | 1 | 1571221.335 | 0.000 | 0.042 | Breaking down Kaesong industrial complex, which is a symbol of the process for peaceful unification of two Koreas, the government of the daughter from the murderous dictator regime allowed the joint military exercise with japan Air Self-Defense Force in Alaska, the US. Does she succeed the pledge of her father, Japanese Dakkakki Masao for Japan? |
| | C****** | 152 | 1 | 498154.435 | 0.000 | 0.009 | News Programs which aired scenes highlighted the darkness of North Korea such as wide-scale of starvation, military exercises in crunch time of Kaesong Industrial Complex; now show us lots of cabs in Pyeongyang streets, fancy women using mobile phones, and hotels full of tourists. |
| | A********* | 104 | 1 | 304125.506 | 0.000 | 0.006 | If S.Korean government had left it was, it would have been operated well. But S.Korean government was mean to Kaesong Industrial Complex and jinxed it, as results 1. sending 6 million dollars, 2. increasing North Korean worker wages also placing additional pressures on South Korean firms, 3. covering the damages of firms during the crunch time through South Korean taxation, 4. dividing once monopolistic North Korean market with China, 5. turning barely put into place. |
| | G********** | 98 | 1 | 251031.293 | 0.000 | 0.006 | Park Geun-hye government that had mentioned to break bad habits of North Korean regime send 6 million dollars to North Korea. Previous |

| Date | ID | In-Degree | Out-Degree | Betweenness Centrality | Closeness Centrality | Eigenvector Centrality | Tweets |
|---|---|---|---|---|---|---|---|
|  | L******** | 70 | 1 | 155142.097 | 0.000 | 0.003 | Roh Moo Hyun government that was blamed severely for giving lots of money to North Korea can be now a role-model of Park's government if North Korea pledge to solve Kaesong Industrial Complex. Bitch! Park Geun-hye sending 6 million dollars to North Korea http://t.co/oBGVq4mP3e Kim Dae-jung and Roh Moo Hyun have been blamed for their North Korean policy, called *Peojugi* (blindly giving money to North Korean). Money sent by Park's government would let nuclear arms in North Korea developed and some of South Korean strategically use security matters. |
| Aug. 23, 2013 | L******** | 123 | 1 | 48601.940 | 0.002 | 0.077 | Byun Hee-jae! He said he is proud of Park Geun-hye because she led to the agreement on Kaesong industrial complex without sending money at the program *Kwaedonanma*. Bastard! Then, how about this? Park's sending 6 million dollars to North Korea, approved North Korean http://t.co/oBGVq4mP3e. |
|  | O***** | 43 | 1 | 2945.251 | 0.001 | 0.035 | RT@Luckyline7: Park's sending 6 million dollars to North Korea Approved North Korea http://t.co/CHdplds9o2. Park had blamed Kim Dae-Jung and Roh Moohyun for *Peojugi* severely. Why? Why did she send money to North Korea? Didn't she make the agreement on Kaesong industrial complex by giving money to North Korea? Miss Park is also pro-North Korean! You guys are dumbhead-reactionaries. |
|  | C********** | 29 | 1 | 15087.641 | 0.001 | 0.001 | Byun Hee-jae! He said he is proud of Park Geun-hye because she led to the agreement on |

| Date | ID | In-Degree | Out-Degree | Betweenness Centrality | Closeness Centrality | Eigenvector Centrality | Tweets |
|---|---|---|---|---|---|---|---|
| | J***** | 21 | 2 | 13189.000 | 0.001 | 0.001 | Kaesong industrial complex without sending money at the program *Kwaedonanma*. Bastard! Then, how about this? Park's sending 6 million dollars to North Korea, approved North Korean http://t.co/oBGVq4mP3e |
| | | | | | | | People who watch the news programs on television will delude themselves into that this world is so wonderful because Park's government has investigated both nuclear scandals and a slush fund of the former president Chun Du-hwan. Also recuperating of Kaesong industrial complex and reunion of separated family has done. On the media, there is only praise for the President Park and bad news are watered down. It is a stuffy situation. |
| | S****** | 14 | 1 | 15055.125 | 0.001 | 0.002 | !http://t.co/gddDy55vXe'' @coreal: Lee Myung-bak's crimes, running away by the inter-Korean summit talks which is failure. Lee Myung-Park Geun-hye government is running away by the inter-Korean summit talks! The ridded election from the mouse and the cock is still ongoing. 6 million dollars to Kaesong industrial complex! |
| Aug. 27, 2013 | O***** | 53 | 1 | 185222.333 | 0.000 | 0.056 | RT@Luckyline7: Park's sending 6 million dollars to North Korea Approved North Korea http://t.co/CHdp1ds9o2. Park had blamed Kim Dae-Jung and Roh Moohyun for *Peojugi* severely. Why? Why did she send money to North Korea? Didn't she make the agreement on Kaesong industrial complex by giving money to North Korea? Miss Park is also pro-North Korear! You guys are dumbhead-reactionaries. |

169

| Date | ID | In-Degree | Out-Degree | Betweenness Centrality | Closeness Centrality | Eigenvector Centrality | Tweets |
|---|---|---|---|---|---|---|---|
| | C******** | 51 | 1 | 98719.111 | 0.000 | 0.035 | Byun Hee-jae! He said he is proud of Park Geun-hye because she led to the agreement on Kaesong industrial complex without sending money at the program *Kwaedonanma*. Bastard! Then, how about this? Park's sending 6 million dollars to North Korea, approved North Korean http://t.co/oBGVq4mP3e. |
| | J****** | 42 | 3 | 88601.875 | 0.000 | 0.005 | RT@sasang64: Is it the thinking of Park's family to make sure not to violate the sanction of the UN Security council prior to the resume Kaesong Industrial Complex? Anyway, they don't want to recover of wartime control from the U.S., and depend on the control of the U.S. Do they want to unify two Koreas? They will ask this agenda to the U.S. the first. |
| | O**** | 36 | 1 | 214288.809 | 0.000 | 0.009 | "@ragayoka:: That's an obvious baloney" "@hkb 2838:Shit Hee-jae, shit on the street!" Byun Hee-jae! He said he is proud of Park Geun-hye because she led to the agreement on Kaesong industrial complex without sending money at the program *Kwaedonanma*. Bastard! Then, how about this? Park's sending 6 million dollars to North Korea, approved North Korean http://t.co/oBGVq4mP3e. |
| Aug. 28, 2013 | C****** | 31 | 0 | 56585.252 | 0.000 | 0.004 | |
| | M********* | 21 | 2 | 1967.333 | 0.009 | 0.122 | Commies congressmen Lee Suk-ki is the member of Unified Progressive Party, under the chairman, Lee Junghee; and they can defect to North Korea via Kaesong Industrial Complex so the inspection should be step up completely. Emergency call number for commie spies, like Lee Suk-ki is ☎111. |

| Date | ID | In-Degree | Out-Degree | Betweenness Centrality | Closeness Centrality | Eigenvector Centrality | Tweets |
|---|---|---|---|---|---|---|---|
| | P****** | 21 | 1 | 2036.333 | 0.009 | 0.074 | Request unlimited RTs. I only concern the state, day and night, 24/7. Defeating commies and protecting the nation. |
| | J*** | 13 | 1 | 132.000 | 0.083 | 0.000 | Commies congressmen Lee Suk-ki is the member of Unified Progressive Party, of which chairman is Lee Junghee and they can defect to North Korea via Kaesong Industrial Complex so the inspection should be step up completely. Emergency call number for commie spies, like Lee Suk-ki is @111. Request unlimited RTs. Every day and every night, concerned the state, defeat commies, protect the nation. |
| | Y********* | 12 | 1 | 150.000 | 0.063 | 0.000 | Board members of North-South Korean Relations Committee asked to Ministry of Unification on Kaesong Industrial Complex, separated families, Mt. Keumgang tourism, DMZ Peace Park, and border regions between two Koreas. Ministry of Unification answered well. The representative of Kaesong Industrial Complex expected to restart Kaesong Industrial Complex in a week. Ministry of Unification arranged the paperwork on making Committee and the date of restart Kaesong Industrial Complex is vague. It might be late. #mokpo. Two Koreas reached an agreement to compose the Common Committee on Kaesong Industrial Complex. According to this agreement, issues on restart and normalization of Kaesong Industrial Complex would be debated at the Committee which both Koreas participated in. S.Korean government suggested the first committee |

| Date | ID | In-Degree | Out-Degree | Betweenness Centrality | Closeness Centrality | Eigenvector Centrality | Tweets |
|---|---|---|---|---|---|---|---|
| | B********* | 10 | 1 | 754.333 | 0.006 | 0.009 | meeting at the Kaesong Industrial Complex on second of next month. http://t.co/iJlJ4MZObq. #kocon Korean Confederation of Trade Unions is a group of a gun! They should be defected to North Korea, and North Korea should employ them as labors of Kaesong Industrial Complex. Conglomerates are afraid of them so they hesitate to increase the employment ... http://t.co/Gs 081A3aIR |

## TABLE 6-31: TWEETS ON MOUNT KUMKANG

| Date | ID | In-Degree | Out-Degree | Betweenness Centrality | Closeness Centrality | Eigenvector Centrality | Tweets |
|---|---|---|---|---|---|---|---|
| Aug. 22, 2013 | U**** | 117 | 2 | 213035.501 | 0.000 | 0.051 | North Korea doesn't have any reason not to accept our offers. S. Korean government said the reunion of separated family is not linked with the resume of Mt. Kumgang tourism superficially, but S. Korean government actually accepted the suggestion in related to hold talks for resume the tour from N. Korea. N. Korea should understand that S.Korean government needs time. |
| | J**** | 107 | 1 | 270709.445 | 0.000 | 0.044 | (Office of Park Jiwon, a congressman) Park Jiwon "North Korea must accept S. Korean government's offer in related to hold the talks on the resume of Mt. Kumgang tourism," Kwang ju, MBC radio, script, http://t.co/cW2yWHke2c. |
| | Y*** | 58 | 1 | 237441.717 | 0.000 | 0.002 | Mt. Kumgang Businessmen Council, the group of investors who invest in Mt.Kumgang tourism, insisted that from 2008 when the tour program stopped to now, the expected revenue loss from |

| Date | ID | In-Degree | Out-Degree | Betweenness Centrality | Closeness Centrality | Eigenvector Centrality | Tweets |
|---|---|---|---|---|---|---|---|
| | P***** | 44 | 1 | 58604.282 | 0.000 | 0.000 | 49 members of the council is about 518 billion won. http://t.co/9LfxlUGt2k. 6 replies related to the president election from the NIS female worker comment: free-welfare affairs; I don't want to visit Mt. Kumgang for my life; the reason why national security laws should be existent; I can't understand people who want the denunciation of national security laws; S.Korean government doesn't have any words to say so; what a waste of tax. Is that an intervention of the president election? |
| | L******** | 37 | 1 | 57672.520 | 0.000 | 0.000 | When a victim was killed by a North Korean soldier in Mt. Kumgang, the Korean Alliance of Progressive Movement said "because Mt. Kumgang is under the regime of North Korea so this accident should be guided by North Korean rules, it is not suitable to distinguish between right and wrong on that issue." Their homeland must be North Korea! |
| Aug. 23, 2013 | U**** | 25 | 1 | 552.000 | 0.042 | 0.184 | Set the reunion of separated families, 100 people, at Mt.Kumgang. Prisons of the Korean war and abduction issues are pending. Generally, North Korean agenda was accomplished. North Korea made a concession on one more reunion of separated families in November. Delaying the date of working level talks after the reunion means North Korea want to tie the issues of the reunion and Mt. Kumgang tourism. |
| | N***** | 13 | 1 | 154.000 | 0.071 | 0.000 | Mt. Kumgang Businessmen Council urges the resume of Mt.Kumgang tourism, "because of 5.24 sanction, the bankruptcy of family occurred." |

| Date | ID | In-Degree | Out-Degree | Betweenness Centrality | Closeness Centrality | Eigenvector Centrality | Tweets |
|---|---|---|---|---|---|---|---|
| | Y********** | 13 | 1 | 220.000 | 0.042 | 0.000 | #KOCON Nuclear bomb will come to S.Korea if money is transferred to North Korea via Mt. Kumgang tourism. http://t.co/X8j6YXFamx http://t.co/fZ5t284ty2 |
| | S***** | 8 | 1 | 42.000 | 0.143 | 0.000 | The reunion of separated families comes from 25 to 30 in next month http://t.co/lrvXUqa WOQ. It's very good news! I want to extend the reunion of separated families by this chance and resume the Mt. Kumgang tourism again! |
| | B***** | 7 | 1 | 106.000 | 0.045 | 0.000 | During paid travel, one of tourists was killed at Mt. Kumgang. We give then a present now. We don't know what will happen in Mt.Kumgang when we visit to North Korea for the reunion of separated family. Kim Jung-il who inherited his father's authority is in charge of killing the tourist. |
| Aug. 27, 2013 | U***** | 33 | 1 | 1922.000 | 0.013 | 0.000 | Set the reunion of separated families, 100 people, at Mt.Kumgang. Prisons of the Korean war and abduction issues are pending. Generally, North Korea agenda was accomplished. North Korea made a concession on one more reunion of separated families in November. Delaying the date of working level talks after the reunion means North Korea want to tie the issues of the reunion and Mt.Kumgang tourism. |
| | W****** | 19 | 5 | 1528.200 | 0.005 | 0.094 | RT@s******: They were my comrades. Moohyun and Daejung are conoes. @l********: the reunion of separated families and the return back of living war prisoners are prior to the resume of Mt. Kumgang tour. RT@w******@l******.#KOCON |

| Date | ID | In-Degree | Out-Degree | Betweenness Centrality | Closeness Centrality | Eigenvector Centrality | Tweets |
|---|---|---|---|---|---|---|---|
| | Y********** | 18 | 1 | 2200.267 | 0.005 | 0.037 | Park's government expects to hold a meeting on the prisoner agenda. |
| | I***** | 18 | 0 | 260.767 | 0.005 | 0.082 | #KOCON Nuclear bomb will come to S.Korea if money is transferred to North Korea via Mt. Kumgang tourism. http://t.co/X8j6YXFamx http://t.co/fZ5t284ty2. |
| | L******* | 13 | 3 | 1145.967 | 0.005 | 0.064 | Politicians who gave tax-payers' precious money to North Korea, traders who enjoyed Sunshine policy, and South Korean tourists who liked Mt.Kumgang can't see the Korean war prisoners who desperately want to come back to South Korea. They have bear regrets. |
| Aug. 28, 2013 | U**** | 33 | 1 | 2742.000 | 0.009 | 0.000 | Set the reunion of separated families, 100 people, at Mt.Kumgang. Prisons of the Korean war and abduction issues are pending. Generally, North Korea agenda was accomplished. North Korea made a concession on one more reunion of separated families in November. Delaying the date of working level talks after the reunion means North Korea want to tie the issues of the reunion and Mt.Kumgang tourism. |
| | W****** | 19 | 5 | 4296.867 | 0.002 | 0.094 | RT@sjr0114: They were my comrades. Mochyun and Daejuna are conoes. @lana3358a: the reunion of separated families and coming back alive of war prisoners are prior to the resume of Mt.Kumgang tour. RT@winsroad@ianyour: #KOCON Park's government expect to hold a meeting on the prisoner agenda. |
| | Y********** | 18 | 1 | 9628.267 | 0.002 | 0.037 | #KOCON Nuclear bomb will come to S.Korea if money is transferred to North Korea via Mt. |

| Date | ID | In-Degree | Out-Degree | Betweenness Centrality | Closeness Centrality | Eigenvector Centrality | Tweets |
|---|---|---|---|---|---|---|---|
| | I***** | 18 | 0 | 458.933 | 0.001 | 0.082 | Kumgang tourism. http://t.co/X8j6YXFamx http://t.co/fZ5t284ty2. |
| | J**** | 16 | 1 | 1306.333 | 0.011 | 0.000 | Board members of North-South Korean Relations Committee asked to Ministry of Unification on Kaesong Industrial Complex, separated families, Mt. Keumgang tourism, DMZ Peace Park, and border regions between two Koreas. Ministry of Unification answered well. The representative of Kaesong Industrial Complex expected to restart Kaesong Industrial Complex in a week. Ministry of Unification arranged the paperwork on making Committee and the date of restart Kaesong Industrial Complex is vague. It might be late. #mokpo |

# Mount Kumkang Tourism

Mount Kumkang tourism, which opened in 1998, used to be yet another symbol of inter–Korean rapprochement. At first, tourists are allowed to visit the mountain inside North Korea by cruise ship only. However, as early as 2002, when a newly built road constructed by Hyundai Group was opened, tourists could visit by bus.

**TABLE 6–32: BRIEF HISTORY OF MOUNT KUMKANG TOURISM**

| Year | Event | Tourists (N) |
|---|---|---|
| 1998 | **June.** Chung Ju-yung visited North Korea through Panmunjom (brought 500 cows) and negotiated the Mount Kumkang tour **Nov.** Launched Mount Kumkang Tourism | 10,554 |
| 1999 | **June.** Shut down the tour temporarily due to detainment of S. Korean tourist **Aug.** Resumed the tour | 148,074 |
| 2000 | **Sept.** Kim Jung-il visited Mount Kumkang | 213,009 |
| 2001 | **Oct.** Both Korean working groups held talks on promotion of Mount Kumkang tour | 57,879 |
| 2002 | **Apr.** Reunion of separated families held at Mount Kumkang | 84,727 |
| 2003 | **Oct.** Overload tour from S. Korea to Mt. Kumgang started | 74,334 |
| 2004 | **July.** Launched a day tour program, opened Hotel Mount Kumkang | 268,420 |
| 2005 | **Aug.** Constructed the reunion center for separated families and equipped facilities (restaurant Okrewkwan, hotel beach, etc.) in Mount Kumkang | 298,247 |
| 2006 | **July.** Opened Hwajinpo-Asan rest area, Hotel Oegeum river | 234,446 |
| 2007 | **May.** Opened Kumkang duty-free shop **June.** Launched NaegeumRiver tour | 345,006 |
| 2008 | **March.** Started car tourism **May.** Opened the Mount Kumkang golf link Ananti **July.** Park Wang-ja, one of the tourists, shot by a N. Korean soldier; S. Korean government shut down Mount Kumkang tour | 199,966 |
| 2010 | **Apr.** N. Korea enforced the N. Korean assets forfeit or freeze (from S. Korean government, Hyundai Asan, other cooperators) | — |

*Source: Ministry of Unification, Unification White Paper, 2014*

In 2008, Park Wang-ja, a 53-year-old South Korean tourist, was shot twice and killed by a North Korean soldier when she entered a military area outside the resort zone, according to North

Korea. South Korea's request for a joint inquiry was denied, and subsequently, South Korea temporarily suspended tours until proper measures could be guaranteed for tourist safety. North Korea expelled the South Korean workers at the resort in August 2008. That is how Mount Kumkang tourism became known as a "fresh supply of dollars" to North Korea because tourists were allowed to use only dollars or Euros.

**TABLE 6–33: SOCIAL MEDIA
ON MOUNT KUMKANG TOURISM, 2013**

| | Date | Mentions | Replies | Tweets | Total |
|---|---|---|---|---|---|
| Mount Kumkang Tourism | Aug. 22, 2013 | 1,422 | 56 | 1,223 | 2,701 |
| | Aug. 23, 2013 | 124 | 4 | 87 | 215 |
| | Aug. 27, 2013 | 320 | 22 | 224 | 566 |
| | Aug. 28, 2013 | 417 | 26 | 331 | 774 |
| | SUBTOTAL | 2,283 | 108 | 1,865 | 4,256 |

**TABLE 6–34: MOST FREQUENTLY MENTIONED WORDS:
MOUNT KUMKANG TOURISM**

| Rank | Aug. 22, 2013 word | N | Aug. 23, 2013 word | N | Aug. 27, 2013 word | N | Aug. 28, 2013 word | N |
|---|---|---|---|---|---|---|---|---|
| 1 | Mount Kumkang | 1,690 | Mount Kumkang | 137 | Mount Kumkang | 322 | Mount Kumkang | 493 |
| 2 | RT | 1,327 | RT | 114 | RT | 289 | RT | 376 |
| 3 | Tour | 1,032 | Reunion | 67 | Tour | 160 | Tour | 248 |
| 4 | Mount Kumkang Tourism | 879 | Mount Kumkang Tourism | 62 | reunion | 105 | Mount Kumkang Tourism | 153 |
| 5 | resume | 597 | Separated family | 49 | Mount Kumkang Tourism | 91 | Separated familiy | 126 |
| 6 | Separated family | 573 | Kaesong Industrial Complex | 38 | Separated family | 87 | reunion | 121 |
| 7 | government | 516 | For reunion | 35 | Prisoners of the war | 75 | resume | 98 |
| 8 | suggest | 357 | newsvop | 33 | Kaesong Industrial Complex | 65 | Kaesong Industrial Complex | 92 |
| 9 | North Korea | 322 | Prisoners of the war | 33 | For | 56 | Government would | 88 |

| Rank | Aug. 22, 2013 | | Aug. 23, 2013 | | Aug. 27, 2013 | | Aug. 28, 2013 | |
|------|---------------|---|---------------|---|---------------|---|---------------|---|
| | word | N | word | N | word | N | word | N |
| 10 | talks | 305 | Reunion of separated family | 31 | Working-level talks | 54 | Government | 80 |

With regard to the resumption of Mount Kumkang tours, social media users demonstrated a cooled-down attitude by making the most tweets, messages and replies on the day of the announcement that working-level inter–Korean talks would be held. The most frequent messages were regarding "separated families" and the "Kaesong Industrial Complex," implying that social media users viewed Mount Kumkang tourism in conjunction with these issues. Some mentioned that the reopening of the tours would provide financial support for the North Korean nuclear project, while others mentioned that POWs and the abduction of South Korean citizens should also be dealt with in the talks.

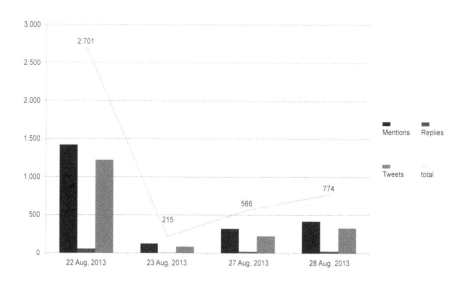

**Figure 6–29: Social Media on Mount Kumkang Tourism**

## The Reunion of Separated Families

Again, social media users were found to regard this issue in conjunction with such issues as Mount Kumkang tourism and the Kaesong Industrial Complex.

When reviewing without the keywords "reunion of separated families," most messages, replies and tweets frequently mentioned issues like Mount Kumkang, Mount Kumkang tours, and the Kaesong Industrial Complex, implying these issues are closely interconnected. In addition, most users linked news reports and mentioned that reunions should be arranged without delay for humanitarian reasons.

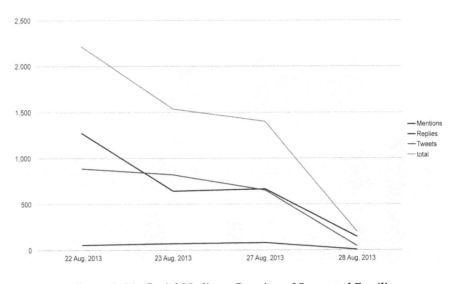

**Figure 6–30: Social Media on Reunion of Separated Families**

TABLE 6–35: BRIEF HISTORY OF REUNION
OF SEPARATED FAMILIES AND CONDITIONS

| Year | Event | Reunion Place | Confir-mation | Exchange Letters (N) | Meeting in S. Korea (N) | Meeting in N. Korea (N) | Video Reunion (N) |
|---|---|---|---|---|---|---|---|
| 1985 | **Sept.** Separated family member visited hometown, and both Korea's art troupes exchanged visits | Seoul Pyongyang | 65 | — | 30 | 35 | — |
| 2000 | **Aug., Nov.** Held 1st and 2nd reunions of separated families | Seoul Pyongyang | 792 | 39 | 201 | 202 | — |
| 2001 | **Apr., Sept.** Held 3rd reunion of separated families | Mount Kumgang | 744 | 623 | 100 | 100 | — |
| 2002 | **Apr.–May, Sept.** Held 4th and 5th reunions of separated families | Mount Kumkang | 261 | 9 | — | 398 | — |
| 2003 | **Feb., June–July, Sept.** Held 6th, 7th and 8th reunions of separated families | Mount Kumkang | 963 | 8 | — | 598 | — |
| 2004 | **March–Apr., July.** Held 9th and 10th reunions of separated families | Mount Kumkang | 681 | — | — | 400 | — |
| 2005 | **Sept.** Held 1st video reunion of separated families and 11th reunion of separated families **Nov.** Held 2nd video reunion and 12th reunion of separated families | Mount Kumkang | 962 | — | — | 397 | 199 |
| | **Dec.** Held 3rd video reunion of separated families | | | | | | |
| 2006 | **Feb.** Held 4th video reunion of separated families | Mount Kumkang | 1,069 | — | — | 594 | 80 |

| Year | Event | Reunion Place | Confirmation | Exchange Letters (N) | Meeting in S. Korea (N) | Meeting in N. Korea (N) | Video Reunion (N) |
|---|---|---|---|---|---|---|---|
| | **March.** Held 13th reunion of separated families | | | | | | |
| | **June.** Held 14th reunion of separated families | | | | | | |
| 2007 | **March.** Held 5th video reunion of separated families | Mount Kumkang | 1,196 | — | — | 388 | 278 |
| | **May.** Held 15th reunion of separated families | | | | | | |
| | **Aug.** Held 6th video reunion of separated families | | | | | | |
| | **Oct.** Held 16th reunion of separated families | | | | | | |
| | **Nov.** Held 7th video reunion of separated families | | | | | | |
| 2009 | **Sept.** Held 17th reunion of separated families | Mount Kumkang | 302 | — | — | 195 | — |
| 2010 | **Oct.** Held 18th reunion of separated families | Mount Kumkang | 302 | — | — | 191 | — |
| 2013 | — | — | 316 | — | — | — | — |
| 2014 | **Feb.** Held 19th reunion of separated families | Mount Kumkang | — | — | — | 170 | — |
| 2015 | **Oct.** Held 20th reunion of separated families | Mount Kumkang | 317 | — | — | 186 | — |

• Registered number of separated families: 130,892 (from 1988 to 31. Aug. 2016)
• The number of survivors: 63,152 (from 1988 to 31 Aug. 2016)
• The number of deaths: 67,740 (from 1988 to 31 Aug. 2016)

*Source: https://reunion.unikorea.go.kr/reuni/home/pds/reqststat/list.do?mid=SM00000129; https:nkinfo.unikorea.go.kr*

## TABLE 6–36: SOCIAL MEDIA ON REUNION OF SEPARATED FAMILIES

|  | Date | Mentions | Replies | Tweets | Total |
|---|---|---|---|---|---|
| Separated Family | Aug. 22, 2013 | 1,272 | 56 | 888 | 2,216 |
|  | Aug. 23, 2013 | 644 | 71 | 822 | 1,537 |
|  | Aug. 27, 2013 | 667 | 81 | 654 | 1,402 |
|  | Aug. 28, 2013 | 148 | 8 | 48 | 204 |
|  | SUBTOTAL | 2,731 | 216 | 2,412 | 5,359 |

## TABLE 6–37: MOST FREQUENTLY MENTIONED WORDS: REUNION OF SEPARATED FAMILIES

| Rank | Aug. 22, 2013 word | N | Aug. 23, 2013 word | N | Aug. 27, 2013 word | N | Aug. 28, 2013 word | N |
|---|---|---|---|---|---|---|---|---|
| 1 | Separated families | 1,638 | Separated families | 1,227 | Separated families | 907 | Separated families | 42 |
| 2 | RT | 1,255 | Reunion | 754 | RT | 603 | Reunion | 21 |
| 3 | Reunion | 866 | RT | 604 | Reunion | 477 | Mount Kumkang | 20 |
| 4 | Accept | 552 | South and North | 550 | First | 225 | Don't do | 7 |
| 5 | Mount Kumkang | 537 | 30 days | 231 | Candidate | 200 | On 23 | 7 |
| 6 | Suggest | 441 | Chuseok | 222 | 500 people | 195 | Kaesong Industrial Complex | 6 |
| 7 | Chuseok | 426 | Reunion of separated families | 205 | draw | 186 | KBS NEWS 9 | 6 |
| 8 | North | 358 | 25 | 202 | South and North | 182 | Q | 6 |
| 9 | Tourism | 343 | At Mount Kumkang | 179 | Will | 130 | News | 6 |
| 10 | Mount Kumkang Tourism | 297 | For reunion | 174 | selected | 116 | visit | 6 |

# Conclusion

This book starts with an objective to demonstrate the correlations between national security and the media in South Korea under the age of social media. It also probes the change social media has brought to the traditional link between the media and national security. To this end, it reviews relevant issues revolving around conflict between national security and civil liberty, the role of the National Assembly and legal judgment over the conflict between civil liberty and national security issues.

There is a brief review on the changes in the debate between civil right and political tolerance for national security at the juncture between democratization, globalization and continued threats from North Korea. This volume explains that South Korean citizens' political tolerance depends on their threat perception on North Korea. In addition, it also shows that the pattern of trade-offs between civil liberty and national security in South Korea has experienced great change as a result of democratization and globalization. Now, personal preference between civil rights and national security is determined by ideological disposition, national pride and individual opinion on North Korea. While conservatives dwell upon worst-case scenarios, liberals do not regard concession in inter–Korean negotiations as a defeat. Citizens' concession of civil rights in the face of North Korea's provocations does not last long, as other events occur and public perception of threats diminishes.

When national security and fundamental democratic values clash, not only the public but also the media face a trade-off dilemma. The clash magnifies ideological conflict and at the same time decreases government influence in controlling the flow of sensitive military information. In this process, more and more actors are invited. What is typical in South Korea is a conspicuous difference between civil liberties at the state level and individual liberty. Surrendering civil liberty for security at the state level does not mean surrender of individual liberty. Security is not in the minds of young voters who usually have "non-attitudes" toward security. To most South Koreans, North Korea's threats and provocations are an immunized item in their trade-off between security and civil liberty. Their individual concern for day-to-day civil liberty significantly differs from their vague concern for broader security issues.

In South Korea, the level of trust in governmental authority, threat perception and personal faith in civil liberty form different public opinions which compete with each other to shape the direction and magnitude of trade-offs between national security and civil liberty. Lack of trust in government dissuades citizens from ceding their civil right even in the face of North Korea's provocations.

In the case of ROKS *Cheonan*, citizens' requests for the right to know more information clashed with government officials' privilege claims that honoring civil rights could result in turning sensitive military secrets over to North Korea. As noted in Chapter 6, military officials filed a request to some members of the National Assembly to explain how their questions and statements during the sessions leaked sensitive military secrets.

Lack of public understanding on the validity of mosaic theory leads to stronger calls for more disclosure of classified information, even though doing so runs the risk of sensitive information falling into the hands of North Korea. Military officials, especially those working in intelligence, put the highest priority on preventing any leak of military secrets. However, doing so increases curiosity and public suspicion among online activists that the government might be attempting to conceal something improper.

Claims and requests to publicize the cross-section of the ship were refused by the navy and the Ministry of National Defense because doing so could inform North Korea about the inner structure of other naval vessels in South Korea which were constructed under similar blueprints. Online activists kept on registering suspicion by stating their version of the sinking that the ROKS *Cheonan* was in fact torn apart after it was stranded on a rock. They criticized the government's decision not to disclose the ROKS *Cheonan,* calling it excessive classification.

This book finds a lack of an appropriate institutional mechanisms for the National Assembly to better position itself between a government watchdog curbing overuse of authority and an amateur in intelligence, leaking sensitive security information. A review of several cases in which mentions and statements by the members of the National Assembly disclosed sensitive military secrets reminds us that the Intelligence Committee in the National Assembly requires institutional redesign. Unauthorized leaks of highly sensitive military secrets during the session and intentional leaks by the members who need public attention for reelection are allegedly used by North Korea.

Under the current structure and composition of rival parties and politicians, military secrecy is very likely to be used as a campaign tool. In addition, high turnover in the membership and a lower chance for influencing members' constituencies mean expertise among members of the Intelligence Committee is harder to achieve. Official pledges of nondisclosure are often reversed because of the "moral obligation" of members to satisfy citizens' right to know. Lastly, a high ratio of National Assembly members who are former journalists is a unique phenomenon in South Korea, implying a closer link between assembly members and the media.

This book also introduces various cases in which the courts made legal judgment over the clash between national security and civil rights. It finds that the South Korean courts have been narrowing the realm of military secrets through the rewriting of relevant laws, thereby seldom respecting the mosaic theory. The

Constitutional Court mentioned that the realm of classification of information should be restricted to the least necessary extent, so that the right to express or the right to know could be guaranteed to the maximum possible degree. The Constitutional Court further mentioned that classification does not mean classified contents should be regarded as military secrets because Articles 2 and 3 hardly seem to bestow almighty and exclusive authority to classify all military affairs.

In fact, among the cases reviewed in this volume, several triggered legal suits. TV coverage of mad cow disease in 2008 was brought to the court for legal judgment. The Supreme Court found MBC producers, who had been charged with distorting public perception on the safety of U.S. beef, not guilty. The negotiated outcome signed by the government also met public dissent propelled by social media. Then, there was a legal case in which citizen activists requested information about the ongoing U.S.–South Korean negotiation over the Free Trade Agreement. As noted in Chapter 3, the Supreme Court ruled that release of information over a negotiation process was not in accordance with national interests. In 2016, South Korea's agreement with the Japanese government over the comfort women issue also encountered strong opposition. It requires further observation whether this opposition will also yield a legal case.

The Constitutional Court called for an effort to form public consensus by pointing out that profit earned from classifying information could not overshadow damage caused by limiting people's right to know. In addition, the court made it clear that public participation contributes to enhanced national security by constructing citizen consensus on important national security policies.

This does not mean the courts in South Korea do not respect government privilege over military secrecy. The courts tend to respect governmental privilege when civil rights clash with classification by the government. The court clearly indicated all information regarding a negotiation did not have to be disclosed even for the purpose of promoting objectivity and transparency. The Seoul Administrative Court ruled that the decision to decline the plaintiff's request was not inconsistent with the Public Information Law because disclosure of information could endanger national security. The court also indicated that lack of transparency could be solved by representatives of the citizens at the National Assembly.

Nevertheless, the chapter registers concern over excessive dependence on legal judgment over national security issues. Legal judgment based on lawfulness and legitimacy could override professional decisions made by intelligence officials with years of experience. Moreover, reliance on legal judgment could conflict with constitutional separation of legal, administrative and parliamentary powers.

As an alternative, the introduction of a regulatory mechanism is suggested. At the same time, courts should be equipped with appropriate security measures to deal with sensitive military secrets because courts that routinely handle classified information will become easy targets for foreign intelligence agencies. Most importantly, it should be noted that professional knowledge and sufficient experience on security affairs are required in dealing with classified documents.

Chapters 4 and 5 demonstrate that the links between the media and national security have taken on a fundamentally new pattern due to the rise of social media. First of all, symbiosis between reporters and government officials is now no longer valid. Social media have enabled each citizen to register his own independent idea, thereby weakening symbiosis between reporters and officials. In this process, the social media gradually are replacing the role of the opinion leaders and elites. As young media users are more accustomed to getting news from social media that provides more behind-the-scenes stories than traditional media outlets, social media take a niche-oriented strategy of attracting a smaller but more loyal audience. As a result, young citizens do not shift their opinions. Rather, they are driven more by opinions and arguments extended in social media. In addition, group psychology in a social media network makes one believe that he or she is supported by many in the group when they post, blog and tweet their personal opinions on national security.

In Chapter 6, various cases are analyzed to show the correlation between the media and national security. In those cases that took place before 2011, the contents of newspaper and TV news are analyzed, with a focus on the comparison of frames between media outlets. Newspapers and TV news demonstrate stark differences in using frames when they cover cases regarding anti–Americanism. Internet TV and online communications are also active. The number of internet TV broadcasts on the import of U.S. beef increased, and the audience size also increased from 240,000 to 1,270,000 within a period of one week.

The chapter also shows that the difference in frames between media outlets is not conspicuous when they deal with issues regarding North Korean provocations. Most media coverage employs conflict and responsibility frames with little variance between media outlets. Social media attention on the issue does not last long, and the number of mentions begins to decrease soon after provocations. Mentions, replies and tweets on inter–Korean relations show that social media distorts humanitarian aid in the form of money transfers to the North by overgeneralizing all types of aid to North Korea. Nevertheless, it is very difficult to clarify the media's causational influence on the actual outcome of national security policies.

The cases of the shelling of Yeonpyeong Island and the sinking of ROKS *Cheonan* demonstrate how the government's official version of what happened was challenged by counterarguments augmented mainly by social media. In the shelling of Yeonpyeong Island, social media users constructed a counter-frame against the official governmental announcement that described the shelling as a North Korean provocation. Social media users argued that South Korea's artillery drills, despite repeated warnings from North Korea, triggered North Korea's shelling.

# Conclusion

Social media tends to show emotional responses to national security issues. In terms of the issues revolving around anti–Americanism, users appear very active in uploading and tweeting opinions. To the contrary, on such issues as missile and nuclear tests which do not influence the daily lives of ordinary citizens, social media demonstrates calm responses without registering consistent interests. When North Korea's provocations have caused direct damage to South Korea, as happened in the cases of ROKS *Cheonan* and Yeonpyeong Island, social media has applied legal procedures for prosecution to prove whether North Korea actually carried out the sinking and whether the shelling was a sort of self-defense measure against South Korea's artillery drill.

Unauthorized disclosure of security-related information has become more and more common. Usually, unauthorized disclosure is meant to publicize wrongdoings by government officials or to warn against the excessive exercise of government authority. Doing so disperses government monopoly of classified information. However, in South Korea, unauthorized disclosure is regarded as an expression of distrust and civil disobedience. Online activists in the case of ROKS *Cheonan* challenged government authority and its monopoly of secrets.

Doing so is not just an expression of distrust against government authority, but rather of disappointment and distrust in the whole political system. It is a challenge against those who are institutionally appointed by elected officials, and thus by citizens. Sagar's quote in Chapter 1 indicates that those who challenge are neither elected by the citizens nor appointed by their representatives. In addition, the media, and more specifically social media, override or replace constitutional procedures such as elections and legal suits, which institutionally determine what is in the interest of national security.

Through constructing challenging frames against official governmental positions, social media performs agenda-setting and priming functions. When national security issues enter the public's perception, they have already been shaped by the gatekeeping and framing functions of the media. Then, by repetition, social media makes a specific case salient and at the same time makes the case understood with little cognitive dissonance. Framed opinions are often the ones that prime people's decisions.

# Chapter Notes

## Introduction

1. Social media is defined here as an information infrastructure to produce and distribute content and a tool to digitalize personal messages, news and ideas. Howard and Parks (2012), p. 362.
2. Baum and Groeling (2010), pp. 6–8.
3. Baum and Groeling (2010), pp. 3–5.
4. Pyszczynski, Greenberg and Solomon (2007), p. 62.
5. Baum and Groeling (2010), p. 29.
6. Baum and Groeling (2010), p. 26.
7. Baum and Groeling (2010), p. 6.
8. Hotchkiss (2010), pp. 367–369.
9. Hotchkiss (2010), p. 369; Swindler (2001); Benson and Saguy (2005).
10. Boulianne (2009), pp. 193–194; Putnam (1995); Alonge (2000).
11. Thorson et al. (2013), p. 423.
12. Tufekci and Wilson (2012), p. 366.
13. Eun-young and Yuri (2012); Rosenberg and Egbert (2011).
14. Edy and Meirick (2007), p. 120; Joseph (2012), pp. 149–150; Madden and Zichuhr
15. Baum and Groeling (2010), pp. 20–22.
16. Lynch (2011), pp. 303–304; Youmans and York (2012), p. 317; Learner (2010), p. 517; Wilson and Dunn, (2011), p. 1260.
17. Wilson and Dunn (2011), pp. 1263–1269; Tufekci and Wilson (2012), p. 367.

## Chapter 1

1. Davis (2007), p. 11 and pp. 29–32.
2. Davis (2007), pp. 6–7 and p. 14.
3. Sagar (2013), p. 93.
4. Davis (2007), p. 12.
5. Davis (2007), pp. 38–39 and p. 61.
6. Davis (2007), pp. 5–6, p. 41, p. 71 and p. 85.
7. Davis (2007), pp. 2–3.
8. Gibson and Bingham (1985), p. 41; Davis (2007), p. 33.
9. Davis (2007), pp. 36–37.
10. Feldman and Zaller (1992); Hochschild (1981), p. 258; Davis (2007), p. 38.
11. Gibson and Gouws (2003); Davis (2007), p. 63.
12. Gibson (1989); Davis (2007), p. 34.
13. Kim (2014), pp. 102–105; Kim (March 2002).
14. Davis (2007), p. 59.
15. Baum and Groeling (2010), p. 29.
16. Entman (2004), p. 107.
17. Pyszczynski, Greenberg and Solomon (2003); Davis (2007), p. 62.
18. LeDoux (1996); Davis (2007), p. 63.
19. Davis (2007), p. 71 and p. 111.
20. Davis (2007), pp. 85–87.
21. Davis (2007), pp. 113–115.
22. Sagar (2013), p. 2 and p. 73, fn. 87.
23. Sagar (2013), p. 3.
24. Sagar (2013), pp. 5–6 and p. 111.
25. Sagar (2013), pp. 113–116.

## Chapter 2

1. Sagar (2013), p. 5 and p. 93.
2. *New York Times,* July 19, 1975; May 4, 1987, p. A1; June 21, 1988, p. A1; Nov. 23, 2003; Sagar (2013), p. 4 and pp. 81–85.
3. For various cases and discussions, see Sagar (2013), pp. 90–97.
4. *New York Times,* July 8, 1941, p. 1; July 25, 1941, p. 1.
5. *New York Times,* Sept. 9, 1974, p. 3; July 9, 1975, p. 38; Sept.30, 1975, p. 23.
6. *New York Times,* July 15, 1987, p. A9; July 16, 1987, p. A8.
7. *New York Times,* July 20, 1998, p. A15.
8. *New York Times,* July 27, 1981.
9. Sagar (2013), p. 93.
10. *Washington Post,* Dec. 2, 2001, p. A25; Davis (2007), p. 21 and p. 23.
11. James Bamford, "The Agency That Could Be Big Brother," *New York Times,* Dec. 25, 2005; Sagar (2013), p. 95.
12. *New York Times,* Sept. 15, 2001.
13. Sagar (2013), p. 82.
14. National Security Agency Law, Article 13, Sections 1 and 2.
15. *Yonhapnews,* Apr. 29, 2015, at http://www.yonhapnews.co.kr/bulletin/2015/04/29/0200000000AKR2015042 9020251014.HTML?input=1195m.
16. *Korea Herald,* May 13, 2015, at http://www.koreaherald.com/view.php?ud=20150513001108 .
17. Sagar (2013), pp. 87–88.
18. *Munhwa Ilbo,* Oct. 6, 2004; *Hangyoreh Shinmun,* Oct. 6, 2004; *Donga Ilbo,* Oct. 7, 2004; *Joongang Daily,* Oct. 5, 2004, at http://koreajoongangdaily.joins.com/news/article/article.aspx?aid=2476923.
19. *Donga Ilbo,* Dec. 7, 2010, p. A4.
20. *Chosun Ilbo,* Apr. 7, 2010, p. A35; *Kyunghyang Shinmun,* Apr. 7, 2010, p. 4.
21. Sagar (2013), p. 90.

## Chapter 3

1. http://www.law.go.kr/LSW/lsInfoP.do?lsiSeq=51985&chrClsCd=010203&urlMode=engLsInfoR&viewCls=engLsInfoR#AJAX.
2. 88-Hun-ma-22 (Constitutional Court Rule, Case No. Ma-22, Sept. 4, 1989).
3. 89-Hun-ka-104 (Constitutional Court Rule 89-Ka-104, Feb. 25, 1992).
4. 92-Hun-ba-6, 26; 93-Hun-ba-34, 35, 36.
5. 98-Nu-8294; 2003-Tu-1370.
6. 97-Ko-hap-149.
7. 97-To-985.
8. 97-To-711.
9. 97-To-1656.
10. *Department of Navy v. Egan* (1988); https://supreme.justia.com/cases/federal/us/484/518/; Sagar (2013), p. 68.
11. 2003-To-5547.
12. 97-No-70; 97-To-1295.
13. 2000-To-1956.
14. https://casetext.com/case/horn-v-huddle-3; Sagar (2013), pp. 78–79.
15. For details on this case, see http://openjurist.org/598/f2d/1/halkin-v-helms-halkin; *Halkin v. Helms,* 598 F. 2d 1, 8 (D.C. Cor. 1978); Sagar (2013), p. 62.
16. Sagar (2013), p. 62.
17. On this case, see Charlie Savage, "Court Dismisses a Case Asserting Torture by CIA," *New York Times,* Sept. 8, 2010; Jane Mayer, "Outsourcing: The CIA's Travel Agent," *New Yorker,* Oct. 30, 2006; Henry Weinstein, "Boeing Subsidiary Accused of Aiding CIA Torture Flights," *Los Angeles Times,* May 31, 2007; Bob Egelko, "Federal Judge Dismisses Suit Over Torture Flights," *San Francisco Chronicle,* Feb. 13, 2008; Joan Biskupic, "Test of 'state secrets' shield goes before Supreme Court," *USA Today,* Jan. 17, 2011; Sagar (2013), pp. 63–65.
18. 94-To-348.
19. 2006-No-185.
20. Sagar (2013), pp. 120–121.

21. http://law.justia.com/cases/ federal/district-courts/FSupp/578/704/ 2363272/; Sagar (2013), p. 59.

22. https://law.resource.org/pub/us/ case/reporter/F2/689/689.F2d.1100.81– 1567.html; Sagar (2013), pp. 76–77.

23. 90-To-230.

24. *United States v. Reynolds*, 345 U.S. 1 (1953); https://en.wikipedia.org/ wiki/United_States_v._Reynolds; Sagar (2013), pp. 59–60; http://www.this americanlife.org/radio-archives/ episode/383/origin-story.

25. http://www.leagle.com/decision/ 1983760709F2d51_1734/ELLSBERG% 20v.%20MITCHELL; Sagar (2013), pp. 77–78.

26. http://www.nytimes.com/ packages/pdf/world/20070303_MASRI. pdf; Sagar (2013), p. 63.

27. http://caselaw.findlaw.com/us- 9th-circuit/1281748.html; https://law. resource.org/pub/us/case/reporter/F3/- 157/157.F3d.735.96–36260.html; Sagar (2013), pp. 69–70.

28. For details, see Sagar (2013), pp. 62–67.

29. 97-Ku-13797.

30. 2007-Ku-hap-31478.

31. 2006-Ku-hap-23098.

32. 2002-Ku-hap-24499.

33. Sagar (2013), p. 104.

34. http://www.boannews.com/ media/view.asp?idx=20516&kind=2.

35. 2005-Ku-hap-3127; 2005-Nu- 22953; 2006-Tu-9351.

36. 99-To-4022.

37. 2011-Ko-hap-1131; 2012-No-805; 2013-To-2511.

38. 2013-To-2511.

39. 2010-No-827; 2010-To-6310.

40. 2010-To-6310.

41. 97-To-1656.

42. Sagar (2013), p. 103.

43. Chesney in Sagar (2013), pp. 65– 67 including fn. 53 and fn. 54.

44. Sagar (2013), p. 70.

45. Sagar (2013), pp. 70–73.

46. 407 U.S. 297 (1972); https://en. wikipedia.org/wiki/United_States_v._

United_States_District_Court; http:// openjurist.org/807/f2d/204/ellsberg-v- n-mitchell; http://caselaw.findlaw.com/ us-supreme-court/407/297.html; http:// openjurist.org/807/f2d/204/ellsberg-v- n-mitchell; Matt Zapotosky, "Ex-CIA officer convicted in leak case sentenced to 3½ years in prison," *Washington Post*, May 11, 2015; James Risen, "Fired by CIA: He Says Agency Practiced Bias," *New York Times*, March 2, 2002; Matt Apuzzo, "CIA Officer in Leak Case, Jef- frey Sterling, Is Convicted of Espionage," *New York Times*, Jan. 26, 2015; Matt Apuzzo, "CIA Officer Found Guilty in Leak Tied to Times Reporter," *New York Times*, Jan. 27, 2015; Matt Apuzzo, "CIA Officer Sentenced in Leak Tied to Times Reporter," *New York Times*, May 12, 2015; Dana Priest, "Wrongful Imprisonment: Anatomy of a CIA Mistake," *Washington Post*, Dec. 4, 2005; Jerry Markon, "Law- suit Against CIA is Dismissed," *Wash- ington Post*, May 19, 2006; Glenn Kessler, "Rice to Admit German's Abduction Was an Error," *Washington Post*, Dec. 6, 2005; Craig Smith, "German Spy Agency Admits Mishandling Abduction Case," *New York Times*, June 2, 2006; Sagar (2013), pp. 66–67.

47. Sagar (2013), pp. 67–68.

48. Sagar (2013), p. 68.

49. http://www.leagle.com/decision/ 19811980655F2d1325_11758/ PHILLIPPI%20v.%20CENTRAL%20 INTELLIGENCE%20AGENCY; Sagar (2013), pp. 75–76.

## Chapter 4

1. Entman (2004), p. 107.

2. Jervis (1976), pp. 172–187; Hindell (1995), p. 73.

3. Hindel (1995), pp. 73–74.

4. Kim (1999).

5. Burt in Serfaty (ed., 1990), p. 140.

6. Graber (1993), p. 26.

7. Hess (1991), p. 109; Mann in Mann (ed., 1990), pp. 1–34; Serfaty (1990), p. 12.

8. Borquez in Spitzer (1993), p. 38.
9. O'Heffernan (1991), p. 82.
10. Hindell (Apr. 1995), p. 77.
11. Serfaty (1990), p. 6.
12. Linsky (1986), pp. 146–147.
13. Graber (2002), p. 173.
14. Iyengar (1991), p. 11.
15. Gamson (1988), p. 166; Kruse (2001), p. 68.
16. Entman (1993), p. 54.
17. Lawrence (2000), p. 93; Callaghan and Schnell (2001), p. 184.
18. Entman (1991), pp. 11–13; *Newsweek* and *Time*, Sept. 13, 1983, issues, Sept. 19, 1983, issues, and July 18, 1988, issues. Entman demonstrated how different words and images chosen by the media to depict similar phenomena revealed differences in "critical textual choices" that framed the stories in different ways..
19. *Joongang Ilbo*, Aug. 7, 1996; *Kyunghyang Shinmun*, Aug. 7 and 8, 1996; *Hankyoreh Shinmun*, Aug. 8, 1996.
20. Chonsun Ilbo, Donga Ilbo, Joongang Ilbo, Hankook Ilbo, Oct. 14, 1996.
21. Iyengar (1991), p. 70.
22. Graber (1989), p. 21 and pp. 338–339; Spitzer in Spitzer (1993), pp. 3–4 and p. 9.
23. Callaghan and Schnell (2001), p. 184.
24. Lawrence (2000), p. 93.
25. Entman (1991), p. 54.
26. Iyengar (1991), p. 83 and p. 130.
27. Kenneth L. Adelman, "Woefully Inadequate: The Press's Handling of Arms Control," in Serfaty (1990), pp. 153–156.
28. Davis (1992), p. 143; Hindell (1995), p. 75; Wallach in Serfaty (1990), p. 83; "McCloskey's Law'" says "the degree to which leaks command and lead the agenda is in inverse proportion to the extent to which government responds to media inquiry openly." For details, see McCloskey, "The Care and Handling of Leaks," in Serfaty (1990), p. 119.
29. Sigal in Manoff and Schudson (eds., 1987), pp. 27–29; Sahr (1993), p 154; Hindell (1995), p. 74.
30. Serfaty in Serfaty (1990), p. 4.
31. *Se-Gye Ilbo*, Feb. 17, 1993, p. 2; *Han-Kook Ilbo*, March 16, 1994, p. 9.
32. For relevant articles, see *Chosun Ilbo*, Jan. 27, 1996; *Hankyoreh Sinmun*, Apr. 24, 1996; *Dong-a Ilbo*, June 8, 1996.
33. Dorman and Farhang (1987), p. 202; Martin and Chaudhary in Martin and Chaudhary (1983), pp. 46–50.
34. Sahr in Spitzer (1993), p. 154.
35. Philip L. Geyelin, "The Strategic Defense Initiative: The President's Story," in Serfaty (1990), p. 28.

# Chapter 5

1. Entman (2004), p. 122 and pp. 165–166.
2. Baum and Groeling (2010), p. 6 and p. 40.
3. Entman (2004), pp. 10–11 and p. 17.
4. Baum and Groeling (2010), pp. 21–22.
5. Entman (2004), pp. 16–17.
6. Entman (2004), p. 73 and p. 114.
7. Entman (2004), p. 18 and p. 120.
8. Entman (2004), p. 49 and p. 74.
9. Baum and Groeling (2010), p. 18.
10. Hotchkiss (2010), p. 369; Swindler (2001); Benson and Saguy (2005).
11. Baum and Groeling (2010), pp. 3–4.
12. Na Eun-young, "Social Media in the Context of Psychology," *Political Communication and Social Media in Korean Society*, XXXX.
13. Baum and Groeling (2010), p. 6.
14. For details, see Baum (2005).
15. Baum and Groeling (2010), p. 26.
16. Jho Chang, ed. (2012), p. XXX.
17. Na (2001), pp. 11¬-13.
18. Hotchkiss (2010), pp. 367–368.
19. Entman (2004), p. 20.
20. Hotchkiss (2010), p. 369.
21. Baum and Groeling (2010), p. 40.
22. Entman (2004), p. 96.

23. Baum and Groeling (2010), p. 29.
24. Entman (2004), p. 95.
25. Na and Cha (2012), p. XXXX.
26. Entman (2004), pp.93–96.
27. "Where are My Friends?" EBS, Apr. 24, 2012.

# Chapter 6

1. Kruse (2001), p. 69; Tarrow (1994), p. 126; Ashley and Olson (1998), pp. 263–264; Parenti (1986); Paletz and Entman (1981); Gitlin (1980); Pan and Kosicki (1993), pp. 55–75.
2. Iyengar (1991); Simon and Xenos (2000), p. 368.
3. Jinwung Kim (1989), pp. 758–759; Clark (1988); Gleysteen in Newsom, ed. (1986), pp. 85–99; Shin, *op. cit.*, p. 793.
4. Shin, *op. cit.*, pp. 794–795; Jinwung Kim, *op. cit.*, p. 762.
5. Seung-Hwan Kim (2002/2003), p. 113.
6. McLeod (1995), p. 4.
7. Moon in Ikenberry and eds. (2008), p. 174.
8. *Ibid.*, pp. 168–170.
9. The three frames are constructed on the basis of the research by Semetko and Valkenburg (2000). For details, see Semetko and Valkenburg (2000), pp. 93–109. In this, the authors use five frames for analyzing 4,123 TV and newspaper stories surrounding the Amsterdam meetings of European heads of state in 1997. They are the frames of attribution of responsibility, conflict, human interest, economic consequences, and morality.
10. Rubin (2002), pp. 80–81.
11. In this study, the term "progressive" includes "leftist" in South Korea's domestic politics and ideological spectrum.
12. MBC *News Desk*, Nov. 20, 2002.
13. MBC *News Desk*, Nov. 22, 2002.
14. According to the Korean Audit Bureau of Circulations, *Chosun Ilbo* records a daily circulation of 2,377,708 papers, while *Donga Ilbo* records 2,051,594 and *Joongang Ilbo* 2,051,588 papers.
15. *Hankyoreh Shinmun*, Nov. 23, 2002; Nov. 29, 2002; Nov. 30, 2002; Dec. 3, 2002; Dec. 16, 2002; Dec. 20, 2002; Dec. 23, 2002; Dec. 30, 2003; Jan. 3, 2003; Jan. 4, 2003; May 27, 2008; June 3, 2008; June 5, 2008; June 7, 2008; June 9, 2008; June 10, 2008; June 13, 2008.
16. *Hankyoreh Shinmun*, Nov. 30, 2002; Dec. 3, 2002; Dec. 11, 2002; Dec. 18, 2002; Dec. 21, 2002; May 10, 2008; May 12, 2008; May 20, 2008; May 21, 2008; June 2, 2008; June 3, 2008; June 7, 2008; June 9, 2008; June 13, 2008; June 19, 2008.
17. *Hankyoreh Shinmun*, Oct. 5, 2002; Nov. 22, 2002; Nov. 25, 2002; Nov. 28, 2002; Nov. 29, 2002; Nov. 30, 2002; Dec. 6, 2002; Dec. 7, 2002; Dec. 9, 2002; Dec. 16, 2002; Dec. 20, 2002.
18. *Hankyoreh Shinmun*, May 5, 2008; May 12, 2008; May 22, 2008; May 26, 2008; June 10, 2008; June 16, 2008; June 18, 2008; June 19, 2008.
19. Korea Press Foundation, *Korean Newspaper Broadcasting Yearbook 2006* [Hankuk sinmunbangsong Yon'gam] (Seoul: Korea Press Foundation, 2006), p. 90.
20. Civil Coalition for Fairness in Media, "Adieu 2008, wishing for world without biased broadcasting" (2008) at <http://www.fairmedia.or.kr/bbs/download.php?uid=51&imgDate=20081222&bbs_code=bbsIdx15>. Accessed March 5, 2009.
21. MBC *NewsDesk*, Dec. 11, 2002.
22. *Korea Herald*, Aug. 22, 2008.
23. *Hankyoreh Sinmun*, June 2, 2008, at http://www.hani.co.kr/arti/society/society_general/291176.html. Accessed Oct. 14, 2016.
24. *New York Times*, July 5, 2006.
25. KCNA, Oct. 9, 2006.
26. North Korea observers mostly indicate three main motives of North Korea's nuclear program: threat perception, prestige of national elites and

domestic interests. For details, see Sagan (Winter 1996–1997), pp. 54–86; Campbell in Campbell, Einhorn, and Reiss (2004), pp. 18–31; O'Neil (2007), pp. 64–65.

27. *New York Times*, Oct. 9, 2006; *Korea Herald*, Oct. 11, 2006.

28. *Korea Herald*, Oct. 11, 2006.

29. *New York Times*, Oct. 9, 2006; *Korea Herald*, Oct. 11, 2006.

30. *Korea Herald*, Oct. 11, 2006.

31. *Korea Times*, May 25, 2009, at http://www.koreatimes.co.kr/www/news/nation/2009/05/113_45606.html. Accessed July 16, 2015.

32. *Time*, May 25, 2009, at http://content.time.com/time/world/article/0,8599,1900828,00.html. Accessed July 16, 2015..

33. CNN, June 12, 2009, at http://edition.cnn.com/2009/US/06/12/un.north.korea. Accessed July 16, 2015.

34. *Time*, Aug. 13, 2010, at http://content.time.com/time/world/article/0,8599,2010455,00.html. Accessed July 16, 2015.

35. *Korea Herald*, Sept. 13, 2010, at http://khnews.kheraldm.com/view.php?ud=20100913000998&md=20100913174943_BL. Accessed July 16, 2015.

36. *Kyunghyang Shinmun*, Apr. 1, 2010, p. 1.

37. *Joongang Ilbo*, Apr. 17, 2010.

38. *Chosun Ilbo*, Apr. 7, 2010, p. A35; *Kyunghyang Shinmun*, Apr. 7, 2010, p. 4.

39. *Donga Ilbo*, Dec. 7, 2010, p. A4.

40. *Kyonghyang Shinmun*, Nov. 29, 2010, p. 2.

41. *Donga Ilbo*, Dec. 1, 2010, p. A31.

42. *Donga Ilbo*, Dec. 7, 2010, p. A4.

43. *Washington Post*, Nov. 23, 2015, at http://www.washingtonpost.com/wp-dyn/content/article/2010/11/23/AR2010112300880.html. Accessed July 16, 2015; *Korea Herald*, Nov. 23, 2015, at http://khnews.kheraldm.com/view.php?ud=20101123001218&md=20101123191336_BL. Accessed July 16, 2015.

44. *Korea Herald*, Nov. 23, 2015, at http://khnews.kheraldm.com/view.php?ud=20101123001218&md=20101123191336_BL. Accessed July 16, 2015.

45. The author is deeply grateful to *Daum* Communications and its staff for their assistance in the collection of Twitter data for this book. Please note that "A reply is a response to another user's Tweet that begins with @username of the person he/she is replying to" and that "A mention is a Tweet that contains another user's @username anywhere in the body of the Tweet." For further information, see https://support.twitter.com/articles/14023#.

# Bibliography

Ampofo, Lawrence, Nick Anstead and Ben O'Loughlin. 2011. "Trust, Confidence, and Credibility: Citizen Responses on Twitter to Opinion Polls During the 2010 UK General Election." *Information, Communication & Society* 14:6.

Anderson, Lisa. 2011. "Demystifying the Arab Spring: Parsing the Differences Between Tunisia, Egypt, and Libya." *Foreign Affairs* 90:2.

Aouragh, M., and Anne Alexander. 2011. "The Egyptian Experience: Sense and Nonsense of the Internet Revolution." *International Journal of Communication* 5.

Ashley, Laura, and Beth Olson. 1998. "Constructing Reality: Print Media's Framing of the Women's Movement, 1966 to 1986." *Journal of Mass Communication Quarterly* 75:2.

Baek, Seon-Gi, and Keum-Ah Lee. 2011. "Media Coverage Patterns of the Sinking of 'Cheonan warship' and their Ideological Implications: A Semiotic Study on the Media Coverage through Baek's Semiotic Network Analysis and Discursive Structure Analysis." *Journalism & Communication* 15:1.

Barry, Jack J. 2012. "Microfinance, the Market and Political Development in the Internet Age." *The Third World Quarterly* 33:1.

Baum, Matthew A. 2005. *Soft News Goes to War: Public Opinion and American Foreign Policy in the New Media Age*. Princeton: Princeton University Press.

Benson, Rodney, and Abigail C. Saguy. 2005. "Constructing Social Problems in an Age of Globalization: A French-American Comparison." *American Sociological Review* 70.

Berinsky, A. J., and James N. Druckman. 2007. "Public Opinion Research and Support for the Iraq War." *Public Opinion Quarterly* 71."

Bissell, Richard E. 1985. "Implications of Anti-Americanism for U.S. Foreign Policy." In Alvin Z. Rubinstein and Donald Smith eds., *Anti-Americanism in the Third World*. New York: Praeger.

Blechman, Barry, and Stephen Kaplan. 1978. *Force Without War: U.S. Armed Forces as a Political Instrument*. Washington, D.C.: The Brookings Institution.

Boettcher, W. A., and Michael D. Cobb. 2006. "Echoes of Vietnam: Casualty Framing and Public Perceptions of Success and Failure in Iraq." *Journal of Conflict Resolution* 50:6.

Borquez, Julio. 1993. "Newsmaking and Policymaking: Steps Toward a Dialogue." In Spitzer ed., *Media and Public Policy*. Westport, CT: Praeger.

# Bibliography

Boulianne, Shelley. 2009. "Does Internet Use Affect Engagement? A Meta-Analysis of Research." *Political Communication* 26:2.

Burt, Richard R. 1990. "The News Media and National Security." In Simon Serfaty ed., *The Media and Foreign Policy*. London: Macmillan.

Callaghan, Karen, and Frauke.Schnell 2001. "Assessing the Democratic Debate: How the News Media Frame Elite Policy Discourse." *Political Communication* 18:2.

Campbell, Kurt. 2004. "Reconsidering a Nuclear Future: Why Countries Might Cross Over to the Other Side." In Kurt Campbell, Robert Einhorn, and Mitchell Reiss eds., *The Nuclear Tipping Point: Why States Reconsider Their Nuclear Choices*. Washington, D.C.: The Brookings Institution.

Campbell, Scott W., and Nojin Kwak. 2011. "Political Involvement in 'Mobilized' Society: The Interactive Relationships Among Mobile Communication, Network Characteristics, and Political Participation." *Journal of Communication* 61:6.

Canes-Wrone, Brandice. 2006. *Who Leads Whom? Presidents, Policy and the Public*. Chicago: University of Chicago Press.

Caplan, Bryan. 2007. *The Myth of the Rational Voter: Why Democracies Choose Bad Policies*. Princeton: Princeton University Press.

Carlin, D. B., et al. 2005. "The Post–9/11 Public Sphere: Citizen Talk About the 2004 Presidential Debates." *Rhetoric and Public Affairs* 8:4.

Charles, A. 2010. "The Politics of Facebook Friendship: The Influence of the Social Structuration of the SNS Upon the Notion of the Political." *Ceu Political Science Journal* 4.

Cho, Hee Jung. 2011. "Middle East Citizen Revolution and the Mediating Role of SNS." *Journal of Korean Politics* 20:1. In Korean.

_____. 2012. "International Comparison of the Social Media Politics:Focusing on Conflicts Between Connection and Disconnection." In Korean Society for Journalism and Communication Studies ed., *Political Communication and SNS*. Paju: Nanam. In Korean.

Cho, Hee Jung, and Sang Don Lee. 2011. "Social Individual and Network Cooperation in the Network Society: Focus on Issue Proposal, Issue Link and Grouping." *Civil Society & NGO* 9:2. In Korean.

Cho, Il Hyoung, Inseok Seo and Gi-Heon Kwon. 2012. "The Effect of SNS on the Electoral Competitiveness: Focusing on the SNS Media Effect." *Chung-Ang Public Administration Review* 26:4. In Korean.

Clark, Donald N. ed. 1988. *The Kwangju Uprising: Shadows Over the Regime in South Korea*. Boulder, Colo.: Westview Press.

Dalton, Russell J. 2008. "Citizenship Norms and the Expansion of Political Participation." *Political Studies* 56:1.

Daniels, Anthony. 2004. "Sense of Superiority and Inferiority in French Anti-Americanism." In Paul Hollander ed., *Understanding Anti-Americanism: Its Origins and Impact at Home and Abroad*. Chicago: Ivan R. Dee.

Davis, Darren W. 2007. *Negative Liberty: Public Opinion and the Terrorist Attacks on America*. New York: Russell Sage Foundation.

Davis, Richard. 1992. *The Press and American Politics*. New York: Longman.

Doeveren, R. Van. 2011. "Engaging the Arab World Through Social Diplomacy." *Clingendael Paper* 4.

# Bibliography

Dorman, William A., and Mansour Farhang. 1987. *The U.S. Press and Iran: Foreign Policy and the Journalism of Deference.* Berkeley: University of California Press.

Downie, Leonard, and Robert G. Kaiser. 2002. *The News About the News: American Journalism in Peril.* New York: Knopf.

Druckman, J. N., and Kjersten R. Nelson. 2003. "Framing and Deliberations: How Citizens' Conversations Limit Elite Influence." *American Journal of Political Science* 47:4.

Edy, Jilly A., and Patrick C Meirick. 2007. "Wanted, Dead or Alive: Media Frames, Frame Adoption, and Support for the War in Afghanistan." *Journal of Communication* 57:1.

Entman, Robert. 1991. "Framing U.S. Coverage of International News: Contrasts in Narratives of the KAL and Iran Air Incidents." *Journal of Communication* 41:4.

_____. 1993. "Framing: Toward Clarification of a Fractured Paradigm." *Journal of Communication* 43:4.

_____. 2004. *Projections of Power: Framing News, Public Opinion, and U.S. Foreign Policy.* Chicago: University of Chicago Press.

Fogel, J., and ElhamNehmad. 2009. "Internet Social Network Communities: Risk Taking, Trust, and Privacy Concerns." *Computers in Human Behavior* 25:1.

Gabrielson, Teena. 2005. "Obstacles and Opportunities: Factors That Constrain Elected Officials' Ability to Frame Political Issues," in Karen Callaghan and Frauke Schnell eds., *Framing American Politics.* Pittsburgh: University of Pittsburgh Press.

Gamson, William A. 1988. "The 1987 Distinguished Lecture: A Constructionist Approach to Mass Media and Public Opinion." *Symbolic Interaction* 11:2.

Garfinkle, Adam. 2004. "Peace Movements and the Adversary Culture." In Paul Hollander, ed., *Understanding Anti-Americanism: Its Origins and Impact at Home and Abroad.* Chicago: Ivan R. Dee.

Gerbaudo, Paolo. 2012. *Tweets and the Streets: Social Media and Contemporary Activism.* London: Pluto Press.

Gibson, James L., and Amanda Gouws. 2003. *Overcoming Intolerance in South Africa: Experiments in Democratic Persuasion.* New York: Oxford University Press.

Gibson, James L., and Richard Bingham. 1985. *Civil Liberties and the Nazis: The Skokie Free Speech Controversy.* New York: Praeger.

Gibson, Rachel K. 2009. "New Media and the Revitalisation of Politics." *Representation* 45:3.

Gitlin, Todd. 1980. *The Whole World Is Watching: Mass Media in the Making and Unmaking of the New Left.* Berkeley: University of California Press.

Gleysteen, William H. 1986. "Korea: A Special Target of American Concern." In David Newsom, ed., *The Diplomacy of Human Rights.* Lanham: University Press of America.

Graber, Doris. 1989. *Mass Media and American Politics.* Washington, D.C.: CQ Press.

Gregory, Bruce. 2008. "Public Diplomacy: Sunrise of an Academic Field." *The Annals of the American Academy of Political and Social Science* 616:1.

# Bibliography

Ha, Sungtae. 2012. "Use of Social Network Service and Socio-Political Interest and Participation." *Journal of Communication Science* 12:4. In Korean.

Hallin, Daniel. 1986. *The "Uncensored War": The Media and Vietnam.* Berkeley: University of California Press.

Hamilton, James T. 2003. *All the News That's Fit to Sell: How the Market Transforms Information into News.* Princeton: Princeton University Press.

Haseler, Stephen. 1986. *Anti-Americanism: Steps on a Dangerous Path.* London: Alliance Publishers for the Institute for European Defence and Strategic Studies.

Hess, Stephen. 1991. *Live from Capitol Hill! Studies of Congress and the Media.* Washington, D.C.: The Brookings Institution.

Hindell, Keith. 1995. "The Influence of the Media on Foreign Policy." *International Relations* 12:4.

Hong, Won Sik. 2012 "A Study of Media Effect on College Students' Voting Participation: Focusing on the Difference Between Mass Media and SNS Use." *Speech & Communication* 18. In Korean.

Hotchkiss, Nikole. 2010. "Globalizing Security? Media Framing of National Security in France and the United States from the Cold War Through 11 September." *International Journal of Comparative Sociology* 51.

Howard, Philip N., and Malcolm R. Parks. 2012. "Social Media and Political Change: Capacity, Constraint, and Consequence." *Journal of Communication* 62:2.

Howell, William, and Douglas Kriner. 2008. "Congress, the President, and the Iraq War's Domestic Political Front." In Lawrence C. Dodd and Bruce I. Oppenheimer eds., *Congress Reconsidered.* Washinton, D.C.: CQ Press.

Iyengar, Shanto. 1991. *Is Anyone Responsible? How Television Frames Political Issues.* Chicago: University of Chicago Press.

Jervis, Robert. 1976. *Perception and Misperception in International Politics.* Princeton: Princeton University Press.

Jho, Whasun. 2012. "Social Network and Political Change." In Dok-jin Chang ed., *With Whom and How to Do Twitter.* Seoul: Hanul. In Korean.

Joseph, Sarah. 2012. "Social Media, Political Change and Human Rights." *Boston College International & Comparative Law Review* 35.

Kaplan, Andreas M., and Michael Haelein. 2010. "Users of the World, Unite! the Challenge and Opportunities of Social Media." *Business Horizons* 53:1.

Kim, Jinwung. 1989. "Recent Anti-Americanism in South Korea: The Causes." *Asian Survey* 29:8.

Kim, Sangbae. 2012. "Social Media and Public Diplomacy: U.S. Strategies from the Perspective of Actor-Network Theory." *The Korean Journal of International Relations* 52:2. In Korean.

Kim, Seung-Hwan. 2002. "Anti-Americanism in Korea." *The Washington Quarterly* 26:1.

Kim, Sung Tae, Yeo Jin Kim, Hong Gyu Choi and Hyoung Jee Kim. 2011. "Communication Channel Expansion and Political Participation: Focusing on the Internet and Social Media." *Peace Studies* 19:1. In Korean.

Kim, Yongho. 1999. *Foreign & Security Policy, the Media and the Parliament.* Seoul: Oreum. In Korean.

\_\_\_\_. 2012. "North Korea's Use of Terror & Coercive Diplomacy: Looking for Its Circumstantial Variants." *Korean Journal of Defense Analysis* 16:1.

\_\_\_\_. 2014. *North Korean Foreign Policy: Security Dilemma and the Succession.* Lanham: Lexington Books.

Kruse, Corwin R. 2001. "The Movement and the Media: Framing the Debate Over Animal Experimentation." *Political Communication.* 18:1

Kull, Steven, and I. M. Destler. 1999. *Misreading the Public: The Myth of a New Isolationism.* Washington, D.C.: The Brookings Institution Press.

Laer, Jeroen V., and Peter Van Aelst. 2010. "Internet and Social Movement Action Repertoires: Opportunities and Limitations." *Information, Communication & Society* 13:8.

Lance, Bennett W., Regina Lawrence and Steven Livingston. 2007. *When the Press Fails: Political Power and the News Media from Iraq to Katrina.* Chicago: University of Chicago Press.

Larson, Eric V. 1996. *Casualties and Consensus: the Historical Role of Casualties in the Domestic Support for U.S. Military Operations.* Santa Monica, CA: RAND.

Larsson, A. O., and Hallvard Moe. 2012. "Studying Political Microblogging: Twitter Users in the 2010 Swedish Election Campaign." *New Media & Society* 14:5.

Lawrence, Regina G. 2000. "Game-Framing the Issue: Tracking the Strategy Frame in Public Policy News." *Political Communication* 17:2.

Learner, Melissa. 2010. "Connecting the Actual with the Virtual: The Internet and Social Movement Theory in the Muslim World—The Cases of Iran and Egypt." *Journal of Muslim Minority Affairs* 30:4.

Lee, J., and Hyunjoo Lee. 2010. "The Computer-Mediated Communication Network: Exploring the Linkage Between the Online Community and Social Capital." *New Media and Society* 12.

Lee, Soo Bum, and Youn Gon Kang. 2013. "A Frame Analysis on Korean Daily Newspapers' Coverage on Twitter: Focusing on the Perspective of Political Communication and Formation of Public Opinion." *Korean Journal of Journalism & Communication Studies* 57:1. In Korean.

Lippmann, Walter. 1920. *Liberty and the News.* New York: Harcourt, Brace, and Howe.

\_\_\_\_. 1922. *Public Opinion.* New York: Macmillan.

\_\_\_\_. 1934. *The Method of Freedom.* New York: Macmillan.

\_\_\_\_. 1955. *Essays in the Public Philosophy.* Boston: Little, Brown.

Lynch, Marc. 2011. "After Egypt: The Limits and Promise of Online Challenges to the Authoritarian Arab State." *Perspectives on Politics* 9:2.

Mann, Thomas E. 1990. "Making Foreign Policy: President and Congress." In Thomas E. Mann, ed., *A Question of Balance: the President, the Congress and Foreign Policy.* Washington, D.C.: The Brookings Institution.

Marlin-Bennett, R., and E. Nicole Thornton. 2012. "Governance Within Social Media Websites: Ruling New Frontiers." *Telecommunications Policy* 36:6.

Marmor-Lavie, Galit, and Gabriel Weimann. 2008. "Intimacy Appeals in Israeli Televised Political Advertising." *Political Communication* 25:3.

Martin, L. John, and Anju Grover Chaudhary. 1983. "Goals and Roles of Media Systems." *Comparative Mass Media Systems.* New York: Longman.

McLeod, Douglas M. 1995. "Communicating Deviance: The Effects of Television

News Coverage of Social Protest." *Journal of Broadcasting & Electronic Media* 39:1.

Messner, Marcus, and Marcia Watson Distaso. 2008. "The Source Cycle: How Traditional Media and Weblogs Use Each Other as Sources." *Journalism Studies* 9:3.

Minogue, Kenneth. 1986. "Anti-Americanism: A View from London," *The National Interest*. 3.

Moon, Katherine H. S. 2008. "Challenging U.S. Military Hegemony: "Anti-Americanism" and Democracy in East Asia." In G. John Ikenberry and Chung-in Moon eds., *the United States and Northeast Asia: Debates, Issues, and New Order.* New York: Rowman & Littlefield Publishers Inc.

Na, Eun-Young. 2001. "A Study on the Influence of Media Character of Mobile Communication on the Selection of Mobile Communication Company: On Personalism, Immediacy and Directness." *Korean Journal of Journalism and Communication Studies* 45:4. In Korean.

Na, Eun-Young, and Yuri Cha. 2012. "Factors Determining Internet Group Extremism: Anonymity in the Civic Forum, Group Mentality in the Network and Personal as Well as Cultural Factors." *The Journal of Korean Psychological Association: Society & Character* 26:1. In Korean.

Nelson, T. E., and Zoe M. Oxley. 1999. "Issue Framing Effects on Belief Importance and Opinion." *Journal of Politics* 61:4.

Nelson, T. E., Zoe M. Oxley and Rosalee A. Clawson. 1997. "Toward a Psychology of Framing Effects." *Political Behavior* 19:3.

Norris, Pippa. 2000. *A Virtuous Circle: Political Communications in Postindustrial Societies.* Cambridge: Cambridge University Press.

"NTT DOCOMO Mobairu Shakai kenkyusho." 2014. *Mobile Communication.* Tokyo: Chuo keizaisha. In Japanese.

O'Heffernan, Patrick. 1991. *Mass Media and American Foreign Policy.* Norwood, NJ: Ablex Publishing Co.

Oishi, Yutaka. 2012. *Sengo Nihonno Mediato Shimin Ishiki.* Tokyo: Mineruba. In Japanese.

_____. 2014. *Mediano Nakano Seiji.* Tokyo: Keishou. In Japanese.

O'Neal, Andrew. 2007. *Nuclear Proliferation in Northeast Asia: the Quest for Security.* New York: Palgrave.

Page, Benjamin, and Marshall M. Bouton. 1994. *The Foreign Policy Disconnect: What Americans Want from Our Leaders but Don't Get.* Chicago: University of Chicago Press.

Paletz, David L., and Robert M. Entman. 1981. *Media, Power, Politics.* New York: The Free Press.

Pan, Zhongdang, and Gerald M. Kosicki. 1993. "Framing Analysis: An Approach to News Discourse," *Political Communication* 10:1.

Parenti, Michael. 1986. *Inventing Reality: the Politics of the Mass Media.* New York: St. Martin's Press.

Park, Sang-Ho. 2012. "Critical Study on the Forming Public Opinion of SNS and Participation Behavior." *Korean Journal of Communication & Information* 58.

Porta, Donatella Della. 2011. "Communication in Movement: Social Movement as Agents of Participatory Democracy." *Information, Communication & Society* 14:6.

# Bibliography

Prior, Markus. 2007. *Post-Broadcast Democracy: How Media Choice Increases Inequality in Political Involvement and Polarizes Elections.* New York: Cambridge University Press.

Putnam, Robert. 1995. "Turning In, Turning Out: The Strange Disappearance of Social Capital in America." *Political Science and Politics* 28:4.

_____. 2000. *Bowling Alone: the Collapse and Revival of American Community.* New York: Touchstone.

Pyszczynski, Tom, Jeff Greenberg and Sheldon Solomon. 2003. *In the Wake of 9/11: the Psychology of Terror.* Washington D.C: American Psychological Association.

Reese, Stephen D. 2001. "Prologue-Framing Public Life: A Bridging Model for Media Research." In Stephen D. Reese, Oscar H. Gandy, August E. Grant, eds., *Framing Public Life: Perspectives on Media and Our Understanding of the Social World.* Mahwah, New Jersey: Lawrence Erlbaum Associates.

Rosenberg, Jenny, and Nichole Egbert. 2011. "Online Impression Management: Personality Traits and Concerns for Secondary Goals as Predictors of Self-Presentation Tactics on Facebook." *Journal of Computer-Mediated Communication* 17:1.

Rubin, Barry. 2002. "The Real Roots of Arab Anti-Americanism." *Foreign Affairs* 81:6

Rubinstein, Alvin Z., and Donald Smith. 1985. "Anti-Americanism: Anatomy of a Phenomenon." In Alvin Z. Rubinstein and Donald Smith eds., *Anti-Americanism in the Third World.* New York: Praeger.

Sagan, Scott. 1997. "Why Do States Build Nuclear Weapons? Three Models in Search of a Bomb." *International Security* 21:3.

Sagar, Rahul. 2013. *Secrets and Leaks: the Dilemma of State Secrecy.* Princeton: Princeton University Press.

Sahr, Robert. 1993. "Credentialing Experts: The Climate of Opinion and Journalist Selection of Sources in Domestic and Foreign Policy." In Spitzer ed., *Media and Public Policy.* Westport: Praeger.

Schultz, Kenneth A. 2001. *Democracy and Coercive Diplomacy.* Cambridge: Cambridge University Press.

Schwartz, Benjamin C. 1994. *Casualties, Public Opinion, and U.S. Military Intervention: Implications for U.S. Regional Deterrence Strategies.* Santa Monica, CA: RAND.

Semetko, Holli A., and Patti M. Valkenburg. 2000. "Framing European Politics: A Content Analysis of Press and Television News." *Journal of Communication* 50:1.

Serfaty, Simon. 1990. *The Media and Foreign Policy.* London: Macmillan.

Shin, Gi-Wook. 1996. "South Korean Anti-Americanism: A Comparative Perspective." *Asian Survey* 36:8.

Sigal, Leon V. 1987. "Who? Sources Make the News." In Robert Karl Manoff and Michael Schudson eds., *Reading the News.* New York: Pantheon.

Simon, Adam, and Michael Xenos. 2000. "Media Framing and Effective Public Deliberation." *Political Communication* 17:4.

Song, Hyojin, and Kyungmin Ko. 2013. "The Quality of Social Network Service (SNS), Political Efficacy and the Acceleration of the Political Participation." *Korean Party Studies Review* 12:1. In Korean.

# Bibliography

Song, Kyong Jae. 2011. "A Study on Political Participation of the Social Network Generation." *Korea and World Politics* 27:2. In Korean.

Song, Tae-Eun. 2013. "The Multitude's Foreign Policy Debates and Its Collective Behavior Through Social Media: The Impact of Changing Communication Environment on the Public's Foreign Policy Attitudes." *The Korean Journal of International Relations* 53:1. In Korean.

Spitzer, Robert J. 1993. "Introduction: Defining the Media-Policy Link." In Spitzer ed., *Media and Public Policy*. Westport: Praeger.

Swindler, Ann. 2001. *Talk of Love: How Culture Matters*. Chicago: University of Chicago Press.

Tai, Chong-Soo, E. J. Peterson and T. R. Gurr. 1973. "Internal Versus External Sources of Anti-Americanism: Two Comparative Studies." *The Journal of Conflict Resolution* 17:3.

Tarrow, Sidney. 1994. *Power in Movement: Social Movements, Collective Action and Politics*. Cambridge: Cambridge University Press.

Thornton, Bruce S. 2004. "Anti-Americanism and Popular Culture." In Paul Hollander ed., *Understanding Anti-Americanism: Its Origins and Impact at Home and Abroad*. Chicago: Ivan R. Dee.

Thorson, Kjerstin. 2013. "YouTube, Twitter and the Occupy Movement: Connecting Content and Circulation Practices." *Information, Communication & Society* 16:3.

Tufekci, Z., and Christopher Wilson. 2012. "Social Media and the Decision to Participate in Political Protest: Observations from Tahrir Square." *Journal of Communication* 62:2.

Valenzuela, Sebastián, Namsu Park and Kerk F. Kee. 2009. "Is There Social Capital in a Social Network Site? Facebook Use and College Students' Life Satisfaction, Trust, and Participation." *Journal of Computer-Mediated Communication* 14:4.

Wallach, John P. 1990. "Leakers, Terrorists, Policy Makers and the Press." In Serfaty ed., *The Media and Foreign Policy*. London: Macmillan

Wilson, Christopher, and Alexander Dunn. 2011. "Digital Media in the Egyptian Revolution: Descriptive Analysis from the Tahrir Data Sets." *International Journal of Communication* 5.

Wolfsfeld, Gadi. 1988. "Introduction: Framing Political Conflict." In Akiba A. Cohen and GadiWolfsfeld eds., *Framing the Intifada: People and Media*. Norwood. New Jersey: Albex.

Yoshitomi, Yasunari. 2014. *Violation of Human Rights on the Internet*. Tokyo: Mineruba. In Japanese.

Youmans, William Lafi, and Jillian C. York. 2012. "Social Media and the Activist Toolkit: User Agreements, Corporate Interests, and the Information Infrastructure of Modern Social Movements." *Journal of Communication* 62:2.

Zaller, John. 1994. "Elite Leadership of Mass Opinion: New Evidence from the Gulf War." In W. Lance Bennet and David L. Paletz eds., *Taken by Storm: The Media, Public Opinion, and U.S. Foreign Policy in the Gulf War*. Chicago: University of Chicago Press.

Zeitzoff, Thomas. 2011. "Using Social Media to Measure Conflict Dynamics." *Journal of Conflict Resolution* 55:6.

# Index

# Index

# Index

# Index

# Index

Paletz, David 13, 15
Palmer Raids 23
parachute journalism 12
Park, Jin 39
parochialism 85
Patriot Act 36
Pearl Harbor 34
Pegasus 40, 156
Pentagon Papers 53, 60
perception 9–10, 15, 18, 20–21, 24–28, 78–9, 88, 92, 96, 101–2, 113, 184–85, 187, 191
Persian Gulf 35
personal faith in civil liberties 28
Phillippi, Harriet 75–76
policymaking 12, 14, 16–18, 26, 79, 81
political culture 16, 98
political engagement 9
political tolerance 20–21, 184
portal site news service 108
post–Cold War 18, 78, 101, 104
posting 111, 118, 128–32
power bloggers 100, 111
preconceived notions 99
presidential special pardon 67
press 81, 83–88, 90, 91, 94–95, 101–6, 110, 118, 157; press-room 81
prime-time news program 127; *see also* Nine News; *News Desk*
priming effect 10, 190; *see also* agenda-setting effect
priority 25, 30, 79
privacy rights 19
Proctor, George 61
*Producer's Notepad* 117; *see also* importation of U.S. beef; mad cow; MBC
professionalism 71, 76
progressive 113–14, 120, 124, 146
proliferation of nuclear weapons 136, 140
pro–North Korea 5–6, 25–26, 46, 87, 145–46, 150–51, 157
Protocol on Textile Rules of Origin 131; *see also* KORUS-FTA
provocation 4–5, 17–19, 21, 24,-27, 89, 101–3, 132, 134, 145–46, 149–50, 157, 184–85, 189–90
public 6, 7, 9–20, 22, 26–30, 32, 38, 40, 43–60, 64–69, 74, 77, 78–90, 92, 94, 96–104, 110, 113–15, 117, 128, 133, 136, 149, 154–57; 162, 190; attention 186; distrust 154, 157; opinion 7, 9–14, 16, 18, 38, 48, 78–9, 88–90, 94, 96–99, 101–3, 128, 185; perception 9, 10, 22, 27, 88, 92, 184, 187
Public Information Act 63, 65, 69

Public Information Law 46, 58, 66, 188
Pyongyang 19, 46, 102–3, 132, 18

Q- sheets 84

radio 79, 106–8, 172.
Rangoon 50
ratification 37, 64, 118, 129–30, 132; *see also* National Assembly
R/D bases 69
real-time search 15, 109
reality 11, 26, 86, 89, 97, 104
reconnaissance helicopters 69
Red Cross 162
red-baiting 98
relations between national security and the media 17
reliability checking 8, 11
repertoire 8, 99; cultural 8
repetition 191
Resource Conservation and Recovery Act 61
Retweet 101, 111, 145–46, 149–50
reunion of separated families 162, 173–75, 177, 180–82
right to know 20, 22, 25, 28–30, 42, 45, 48, 58, 64, 76–77, 185–87
Risen, James 74
Rockefeller, Jay 36
Rodong missiles 133
Roh, Moo Hyun 118, 136, 149, 168
Roh, Tae Woo 79
Roosevelt, Franklin D. 23
rumor 57, 101–103, 153–54, 160
Rumsfeld Commission 35
Russia 38, 136, 150

SADARM bullet 49,
Sagar, Rahul 2, 29
satellite 136, 146, 149; military 41; observation 42
SBS 118, 122, 133–34, 137–38, 1441, 143, 147, 151–52, 158–59
Scalia, Antonin 33
Scud-C-type missiles 133
search box 109
secret 17, 29–30, 32–61, 63–64, 68–70, 72–77, 79, 87–88, 102, 146, 155, 157, 185–88, 190
secret privilege 49–55, 58, 60–61, 63, 72, 74
Secret Service 51
self-censorship 22
self-propelled artillery 69
self-reliant defense 135
self-restraint in reporting 96

# Index

# Index